How History Repeats Itself and Why It Matters for Today's Investors

Free Bonus from Captivating History: History Ebook

Hi History Lovers!

My name is Matt Clayton, and I'm the creator of Captivating History. First off, I want to THANK YOU for reading our books in the Captivating History series. As an avid reader of History myself, I aim to produce books that will hold you captive.

Now you have a chance to join our exclusive history list so you can get the ebook below for free as well as discounts and a potential to get more history books for free! Simply click the link below to join.

P.S. If you join now, you will also receive a free Mythology book. Remember that it's 100% free to join the list.

Captivatinghistory.com/ebook

Also, make sure to follow us on Facebook, Twitter and Youtube by searching for Captivating History.

Table of Contents

Introduction

Take the money in your wallet and invest it in your mind. And in return, your mind will fill up your wallet. - Benjamin Franklin

Karl Marx said that history repeats itself, first as tragedy, then as farce. (Perhaps you could say first as Karl Marx, then as Groucho Marx.) But the idea that it only repeats itself twice is a wild underestimation. In fact, it keeps on and on, and on and on, repeating itself. Investment booms and busts happen on a regular basis; bubbles and booms are followed by the inevitable reckoning.

History repeats itself partly because the circumstances are slightly different every time. The fundamentals behind the technology boom of the late 1990s were different from those behind the Wall Street Crash or the South Sea Bubble, for instance. That gives snake oil salesmen the chance to say, "It's different this time" (though the basic pattern is very similar), and it forces analysts to look at the causes and effects of patterns in great detail.

But history also gets the chance to repeat itself because most people lack a grasp of historical facts and processes, thus failing to learn from past mistakes. That doesn't just apply to retail investors; economists, central banks, and professional investors are just as likely to fall into the trap. Again and again, investors make the same deadly mistakes.

History repeats itself because the basic underpinning processes are the same and are based on natural human behaviors and emotions. Everyone wants to increase their wealth, but most people are also worried about losing their money. Their behavior will reflect whether greed or fear has control of their feelings at that particular moment. So, during a boom, many people are happy to go along with the trend, but as soon as the market starts crashing, they panic and sell. It happens time and time again.

The good news is that the more you learn about these cycles, the better equipped you are to spot them. This book will talk about individual historical events, but it will also try to trace the processes behind them and give you an idea of how to spot a bubble in formation.

Unlike many books covering this area, this isn't a book for specialists and economists. You won't need a degree in economics or an understanding of investment markets to get started. It won't use unfamiliar jargon. If technical language is necessary, it will be fully explained.

It's tempting to treat bubbles and crashes anecdotally. They're always dramatic and often feature larger-than-life characters and outrageous stories. But while a good story is always fun, this book will try to draw the moral of the story and give you the ability to develop an instinct about when things are getting dangerously overheated or when you're being sold a confidence trick.

This book is comprehensive. You'll learn about African and Chinese emperors, the California Gold Rush, how ancient Rome and Egypt managed their wealth, why the Dutch fell for tulips in such a big way, why a maharaja's decision to build schools rather than buy elephants is still affecting South India's economy a hundred years later, and how South American silver ruined the Spanish economy. And, of course, we will cover the Wall Street Crash and the Great Recession, as well as the most recent market crashes and the prospects for cryptocurrency.

You'll be taught how to relate the present to the past; for instance, you will be able to compare cryptocurrency with the California Gold Rush or with the Mississippi Company that nearly bankrupted Louis XV's France. The same patterns recur. And what many books on boom and bust cycles don't tell you is that some people manage to make money out of the cycle—sometimes in quite surprising ways.

One of the great things about understanding so many different historical episodes is that you'll be able to see what genuinely is different this time around and what isn't. People who expect every stock market crash to be 1929 all over again or every war to be WWII are inevitably wrong, but that's what happens when you only know two stories and not the underlying reasons behind them.

The way history works is predictable, and it's a secret hidden from most people. It's a secret hiding in plain sight, but most investors prefer anecdotes and thrills to actually understanding the real forces at work. Wise investors, though, think deeply, read widely, and discover those forces and their operations through time. They are then prepared to grow their wealth when the opportunity arises and protect it when necessary.

Chapter 1: Bubbles Are Made to Burst

"I'm forever blowing bubbles,
Pretty bubbles in the air,
They fly so high, nearly reach the sky,
Then like my dreams they fade and die."
Anthem of British soccer team West Ham United

The term "bubble" for an exuberant investment market was invented in the 1700s, and that's no coincidence. Early capitalism was just beginning to mature, with Europe moving from the age of feudalism and absolutism toward a different future. Resources began to move from the royal courts to the cities and, in particular, the banks.

That had been happening for some time. You can see the first glimmer of it in the stained glass of Chartres Cathedral in France, where little figures of guild members—carpenters, masons, bakers, and fur sellers, among others—replace the expected noblemen and royal donors at the bottom of the window. In northern Italy, towns had secured self-government, and banks were being set up in the 1400s that could work on a European scale, lending money to hard-up royalty in other countries.

Furrier's guild, Chartres Cathedral.
MOSSOT, CC BY-SA 3.0 <https://creativecommons.org/licenses/by-sa/3.0>, via Wikimedia Commons: https://commons.wikimedia.org/wiki/File:Chartres_- _Vitrail_de_1%27Histoire_de_saint_Jacques_le_Majeur_-_Fourreurs.JPG

Capitalism got a huge boost from the discovery of the Americas. Everyone knows how Columbus's voyage of 1492 changed the world, but few people know that it was largely responsible for wrecking the Spanish economy. Even though the legendary gold mines of El Dorado were never discovered, huge amounts of silver flowed from South America into Seville. Since it wasn't invested in a productive capacity—Spain was still largely an agrarian economy— that silver simply created inflation. Prices rose as the new silver money chased the same supply of basic goods.

The effect wasn't limited to Spain. At the time, the Spanish Empire controlled much of what is today Belgium and the Netherlands. Spain also ran an increasing trade deficit with other countries, and on top of that, it had a series of wars to finance. By the end of the 16th century, Spain had gone bankrupt three times. Having expelled its Jewish and Muslim inhabitants, it got rid of some of the most skilled and productive members of its population, exacerbating its problems. Most hidalgos (nobility and gentry) weren't interested in trade.

Inflation damaged those who lived on fixed incomes. The lower clergy, government officials, and small landowners saw prices rise while the rents they received were largely fixed. But for merchants, who could stock up on goods at sale prices and sell them for higher prices later on, times were good.

Now, we will look north from Spain to Antwerp, Belgium. This city became the main clearing house for Spanish investments, and it incorporated a number of financial innovations that had started elsewhere. In the Early Middle Ages, one had to trade coins for physical goods; there were no checks (cheques), bankers' drafts, or futures markets. (Futures markets let you buy or sell a commodity at a set price for delivery on a future date. For instance, if you're a farmer, you could sell your crop now and lock in the price, though, of course, you would lose any profit if the market price rose by the time your harvest was ready.) But by this stage, bankers in Italy had come up with innovations like letters of credit, which enabled merchants to send money over long distances without the risk of carrying their funds in silver or gold.

A letter of credit lets you arrive at your destination and get money out of a bank there. In terms of its effects on traveling merchants, it was a bit like Western Union today. But to invest in a venture, such as a trading voyage, you still had to set the whole thing up from scratch each time. That was hard work, and it was also high risk. And since it was difficult to sell a share in a boat that was already halfway to China, you had a problem if you needed money before the voyage was completed.

Enter the joint stock company in the 1550s, and the problem was solved. The joint stock company has been around ever since—it's the basis of modern corporations. It enabled trading ventures to access capital and enabled investors to buy discrete units of stock rather than have to participate actively in a venture. By 1600, it had become the preferred way of setting up new ventures, such as the (British) Honorable East India Company and the Dutch East India Company (or VOC from its name in Dutch). Investors could easily subscribe to new ventures, trade their shares, and get regular dividend payments as a return.

That's over a hundred years of history compressed into a few paragraphs, so it has, inevitably, been simplified. But in about 1600, the state of play can be summarized briefly as this: a lot of money looking for returns and the creation of liquid markets (that is, markets in which it was easy to buy and sell investments) accompanying a period of expansionism. The Dutch, English, and French all colonized parts of the Americas, and the Dutch and English traded with India, Indonesia, and China.

Enter the tulip.

This little flower originated in the mountains of Kazakhstan in Central Asia. Discovered by the Ottoman Turks, it became the height of fashion in Istanbul under Sultan Suleiman the Magnificent. Suleiman often gifted tulip bulbs to deserving officials or foreign ambassadors. Ogier Ghiselin de Busbecq, the Holy Roman emperor's ambassador, came into possession of a number of bulbs, which he passed on to a friend in the Netherlands, Charles Clusius, a doctor and botanist who started breeding them in the botanical garden in Leiden. At the time, this was the only place in Europe where tulips grew.

Clusius worked out how the "breaking" virus could make tulips flare out in extraordinary patterns of variegated color. He was a botanist, not a speculator, and most collectors were interested in tulips for either botanical or aesthetic reasons.

Semper Augustus tulip.

But as always happens, at some point, people began to realize that this rare plant could be worth spectacular amounts of money. Tulips don't breed fast. It takes a couple of years for the offspring from one bulb to be ready to sell, so there was no chance that production could catch up with the market. And while regular-colored tulips were relatively inexpensive, the "broken" tulip strains like Semper Augustus could fetch very high prices indeed. At the top of the boom, a single bulb of Semper Augustus could buy you a mansion on the Prinsengracht canal in Amsterdam.

The bubble really kicked off in 1634, three decades after Clusius had started breeding tulips. By the end of 1636, prices rocketed. Switser bulbs, a popular variety, went from 125 florins a pound to a high of 1,500 florins a pound in just two months.

And then, in February 1637, something happened. No one is sure what it was. One story is that some bulbs not only failed to sell at an auction for their starting price but failed to sell at all. Once the story became widespread, buyers started refusing to pay for bulbs they'd bought already, and tulip prices crashed.

Was this a major investment bubble? Probably not. You could look at it as more like the craze for Beanie Babies. Former General Hospital star Chris Robinson blew $100,000 picking up the toys due to their value as collectibles and went bankrupt in 1993. The US economy, as a whole, did not appear to notice.

In fact, Tulipmania was probably less dramatic than it sounds. Most of the investors were merchants, traders, and the wealthy middle class, so they relied on other sources for funds, not just tulip speculation. Ten years later, many of the tulip sellers were still in business. Just a few of them had been bankrupted by the crash. And the Dutch economy continued to grow.

But it's interesting to look at how the bubble evolved. The early adopters, botanists, and scholars came first. They formed a tight network, initially developing new tulip breeds out of interest. They gave, shared, and sometimes even sold their bulbs. Then, tulips became a little more common, and more people wanted them for their gardens. Tulips aren't easy to breed (two years as offsets from the bulbs and then five to ten years from seed), so there was a limited supply. Prices naturally rose.

At this point, a whole lot of middle-class Dutchmen had an "Aha!" moment and realized they could make a good return by investing in the bulbs. They started getting their deals notarized and arranged ways so the buyers could verify what variety they had bought. (All tulips look the same, except for the couple of weeks a year that they're in bloom.) The Dutch were, after all, already well used to taking risks. Their Baltic grain trade used futures contracts, and what could be riskier than sending a ship out to the Far East for spices or out to the Americas?

So, during the 1620s, tulips became well known as both an investment and one of life's little pleasures. Still-life painters churned out thousands of pictures with tulips in them; the same people who bought the tulips often bought the pictures. And, inevitably, people began to get greedier and greedier. And then, after that failed auction, they suddenly became very scared.

That's the standard process. There is the development (a tulip, the steam engine, the internet, etc.), the pilot projects and early adopters, wider use with the start of an investment market, speculation, an ever-accelerating boom in prices, and then the crash.

And by the way, Tulipmania actually turned out to be good for the Dutch. Now, tulips are as much part of Dutch life as windmills or clogs, if not more. The Netherlands has a huge flower industry, with a global market share of over 70 percent.

The Mississippi Company and the South Sea Bubble

You've probably heard of the Sun King, Louis XIV of France. He built the Palace of Versailles and was responsible for the flourishing of French art and music and the beginning of the luxury trade that is still a big part of French industry. He also had grand designs on the rest of Europe, which meant wars—expensive wars. When he died in 1715, luxuries and wars had nearly bankrupted France. That left his successor, Louis XV (or rather the regent, for Louis was only five at the time), with a problem.

Britain had also been fighting in the same wars as France, and the effect on the British budget had been similar. This created the need for both countries to find some way to reduce the effect of government indebtedness, which had become much too high. And in both countries, private companies offered a way for the government to take advantage of investors' hunger for better returns.

In France, émigré Scotsman John Law convinced Louis XV that his monetary theories could transform the government's finances. In 1715, he set up the General Private Bank, which became the Royal Bank in 1719. He gifted shares to French nobles to ensure their support, and he enabled new shareholders to buy in with only a 20 percent down payment. This vastly increased the bank's capital, which was used to issue bank notes.

Unusually for the time, it was what is now called a fractional reserve bank; that is, its notes were only partly backed by gold or silver reserves. However, its notes promised that the holder could redeem their value against those reserves. And the bank was issuing more and more paper money. That led to high inflation in France, to which the government responded by issuing even more paper money. This cycle would be ruinous unless it could be stopped.

Law's next idea was to create huge state monopoly companies. He acquired the Mississippi Company, which held a monopoly on the French tobacco and slave trade. He then began to promote Mississippi Company shares; investors could exchange their low-return French government bonds (billets d'état) for stock in the booming company. Again, he allowed shareholders to acquire shares for a small down payment, with the remainder due in a certain number of monthly payments. The company then lent the French government money, helping it pay down more of its expensive debt.

The shares rocketed. They were issued in 1719 at five hundred livres for only seventy-five livres down. Within a month, they had doubled in price. And by the end of 1719, they had risen to ten thousand livres.

Law had some good economic ideas. For instance, he abolished internal road tolls to stimulate the economy, encouraged the starting of new industrial enterprises, and revived overseas commerce. But unfortunately, his linked bank and company were fatally flawed by the promise to repay, making them, in effect, a confidence trick. Law seems to have worried about the high prices, trying to engineer a gentle decline in the Mississippi Company share price, but he lost control. Prices fell dramatically, and a run on the bank began. This means holders of bank notes wanted to redeem them in gold. Since only a fifth of the paper money could actually be redeemed, Law had a problem.

At the end of 1720, Law fled France, leaving behind his twenty-one châteaux. He spent most of the rest of his life using his mathematical skills as a card counter in the casinos of Venice, Rome, and Copenhagen. He died a poor man.

Britain had the same problems as France. Government debt by 1720 stood at over £15 million, mostly represented by annuities at 7 percent and a significant proportion at 9 percent. Any attempt to pay the annuities off was opposed by the investors; where else could they get such good returns? The answer came with the offer to exchange the debt for shares in the South Sea Company.

The South Sea Company had practically no assets, but there were plenty of rumors about how it was going to be given a government monopoly or buy another company. The promoters ensured there was a liquid market for the shares, and they made it very easy to buy them. Shares could be bought on credit and were sold for a small down payment, with the rest of the subscription price payable over a long period of time. (A subscription price is similar to a Kickstarter project; subscribers would pay in advance before the project is released.) They also created what nowadays would be called FOMO (fear of missing out) by issuing the shares in tranches at ever-increasing prices. Investors who didn't buy any of the first tranches saw the price rise, and when the second subscription began, they were keen not to miss their opportunity.

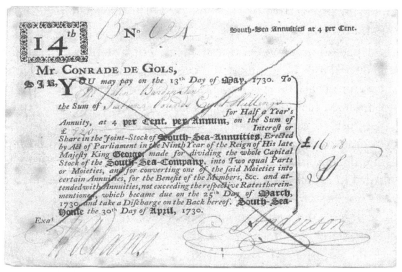

Annuities notice form printed by the South Sea Company.

Other companies were also formed at this time to take advantage of investors' interests. Many were purely speculative.

In fact, very few people appeared to understand what they were investing in. Lord Hutcheson published Some Calculations and came to the conclusion that the shares were vastly overvalued, but even he seems to have overestimated the intrinsic value of the company. In 1720, the shares started at £126 and then shot upward, peaking at £1,100. Of course, it didn't last. By October, the shares were back to £126.

However, the government had gotten what it wanted. Eighty percent of those expensive annuities had been converted into South Sea Company stock, and government debt was back under control. Early buyers of the stock were back where they had started; those who had bought later on lost their money.

The impact of the crash was much worse in France. The Bank of England had kept carefully away from the South Sea Company, so even though there was a stock market collapse, the pound sterling was never in danger. Investment in the bubble had also been relatively limited, with only the upper middle class involved in investment. Most investors lost liquid funds (assets that can be easily converted into cash within a short period of time) but retained business or land holdings.

In France, the fact that the Mississippi Company had become so entwined with the General Private Bank, which was effectively France's central bank after it got royal backing in 1719, had a major impact on the economy. The bubble destroyed public confidence in paper currency and in the government. In fact, some historians believe it was the first in a chain of events leading to the French Revolution. This was a problem foreseen by banker Richard Cantillon at the time. The money supply had doubled, but the economy had not. That money would inevitably be devalued. Cantillon made a bet against his own country's currency and won. But France was back where it had started, effectively bankrupt, but now with a lot of disgruntled citizens who had lost money.

One interesting fact about the South Sea Bubble is that politicians who were privy to the way the scheme worked bought 14 percent of the first two tranches but much lower portions of the next two subscriptions. They were obviously well informed. One way of spotting the end of a bubble is to watch the insiders and notice when they start to move out.

That was certainly the case with the tech bubble and crash. Between September 1999 and July 2000, insiders at dot com companies sold $43 billion worth of stock. That was double the rate of insider selling in the previous two years. A lot of them were out of the market or had banked significant profits by the time the market peaked in March 2001.

Would you have spotted the problems with the Mississippi project or the South Sea Company? One thing that's obvious looking back is that neither company had profitable operations; they were based on the grant of a monopoly but one that had not been exploited.

That's relevant to a recent bubble, the SPAC (Special Purpose Acquisition Company) boom of 2019–2020. The idea of a SPAC is that instead of buying shares in an operational business on the stock exchange, investors can subscribe to shares in a SPAC that will, after it has been funded, buy a business in a particular sector. That's reminiscent of the (admittedly apocryphal) company promoted during the South Sea Bubble, which lured investors with the promise of "an undertaking of great advantage, but nobody to know what it is."

Like the South Sea Bubble, SPACs benefited their sponsors greatly, giving them free shares once they found the right acquisition. They also sidelined SEC (US Securities and Exchange Commission) regulations in an intriguing way. Since they did not actually operate any businesses, they could give "illustrative" financial estimates, something like the serving suggestions shown on food packages. They told cool stories about electric vehicles, rocket ships, 3D printing, and life sciences.

Also, like the South Sea Bubble and the Mississippi Company, SPACs attracted shareholders with a special price break. In the case of the two 18th-century companies, it was a down payment or an attractive exchange for other financial instruments. In the case of SPACs, it was a two-year limited life, after which shareholders would be paid back if the company had not found an acquisition target.

According to Statista, fifty-nine SPACs were floated in 2019. In 2020, the number rose to 248 and then to 613 in 2021. Unfortunately, every SPAC that has made an acquisition (and many are still looking) seems to have missed its earnings expectations. One electric vehicle SPAC, Electric Last Mile Solutions, has declared bankruptcy. Investment bank Goldman Sachs has exited most of its SPACs. And US exchange-traded funds focused on SPACs have fallen between 40 percent and 77 percent from their highs.

Jack Raines of the Young Money blog says of the SPAC frenzy. "When everyone is getting ridiculously rich, everyone takes on ridiculously high risks." That's the way a bubble works—after seeing someone else's wealth, investors discount the risk that comes with it. There's a lesson to be learned there.

Cryptocurrency may well be a bubble. It's quite ironic that an investment that bases much of its appeal on the idea that "fiat money" (paper money that isn't backed by gold reserves) is a confidence trick has, itself, no asset backing or way to demonstrate its value. Right now (summer 2022), cryptocurrencies are crashing. Bitcoin has more than halved from its December 2021 peak, Dogecoin is down from $0.52 to $0.065, and stablecoin Luna has failed after its value dropped from $20 billion to close to zero in a few days. (If the crypto jargon has you reeling, don't worry; there will be a lot more detail on it in a future chapter.)

By the way, never think you are so clever that investment fraud can't deceive you. Sir Isaac Newton lost a lot of money in the South Sea Company. Not only was he a great scientist and mathematician, but he was also a former Master of the Royal Mint. He had a great deal of experience in investigating counterfeit money and other frauds. "I can calculate the motions of the heavenly bodies," he is supposed to have said, "but not the madness of people."

Those were the first three bubbles of early capitalism, and the bubbles never stopped. There was the 1880s Australian land bubble, a railway bubble in Britain, the Roaring Twenties stock market boom (and subsequent Wall Street Crash), the 1990s tech boom, and even the Birmingham Bicycle Bubble! (That was quite a small, local bubble in the West Midlands, England, which is probably why you have never heard of it. Once upon a time, bicycles were the new technology.)

And every bubble ended with a crash—eventually. Because of the huge number of investments piled into a bubble, it never simmers down, as John Law found out. They are all part of a cycle. Although it isn't always easy to see where you are in the cycle, economies follow cycles in just the same way that nature follows the cycle of the seasons.

Former British Premier Gordon Brown famously promised "No more boom and bust," setting out a stable economic policy that was supposed to give his country long-term growth. It didn't work out; the UK was caught in the collapse of the great US subprime boom. Brown failed to win a majority in the next election and stood down as leader of his party. The cycle of boom and bust had had its revenge.

Historians often look at individual bubbles separately. You might be wondering how land speculation in 1880s Australia could have anything in common with the Dutch tulip bulb frenzy or the fortunes made and lost in cryptocurrency. But the formation of bubbles is a natural process, and it has its roots in human psychology: in greed, the fear of missing out, the desire not to "rock the boat" or to look stupid, and perhaps, above all, our love of a good story.

Chapter 2: Investment Disasters: How They Happened and How to Avoid Them

"Speculation building on itself provides its own momentum." -JK Galbraith

We have had a look at bubbles, how they work, and the common features that they share. But you might be thinking about whether you'd be able to avoid being caught in a bubble. The mere fact that a market is trending upward doesn't make it a bubble. Over time, stock markets tend to go up as the economy grows. In this chapter, we're going to look at investment disasters of different types and try to figure out how people could have avoided them by asking the right questions, carrying out the right research, or investing differently.

By the way, one concept that is interesting to look at in this regard is mean reversion. This theory says that while in the short- and medium-term performance may be varied, over time, returns will tend to revert to the average. You can apply this to profit margins; a company can be highly profitable if it is the first mover in a new market, but over time, other businesses will catch up, and the original company's profitability will fall toward average levels. Or you can apply it to stock prices, stock market returns, and price/earnings ratios, the main way that market participants value shares.

Mean reversion works best when it's applied to extreme cases. For instance, let's say the major automakers—Ford, GM, and Stellantis (formerly Chrysler)—are priced at ten, eleven, and twelve times earnings against a historic mean of eleven; there's no benefit in trying to take advantage of the small differences between them. But if they have pretty similar outlooks and yet two of them trade on six times earnings and the other on twenty-four times, then you might want to think about selling the more highly valued and buying the others since you are looking for the ratings to trend back to eleven in the long term.

These stories are not just about stock market bubbles. Some are about individual stocks or individual countries. What they have in common is that they all show how investors, who perhaps didn't understand the basic issues, took a far too optimistic view of an investment and eventually lost their money.

Well-known fund manager Peter Lynch says, "Containing losses is a big contributor to investment success." That's why considering disasters for shareholders and how you might have seen them coming is so useful. If you can avoid making a significant loss, you have already improved the returns on your investments significantly!

The Nifty Fifty

In the 1960s and 1970s, equity investors sought out blue chip, large-cap stocks on the New York Stock Exchange. These stocks were considered to be from highly successful businesses with solid earnings growth and impregnable barriers to entry. The idea of many investors was to "buy and hold forever." Because of this, the Fifty were referred to as "one-decision" stocks.

By the way, the term "blue chip" is quite interesting. Nowadays, it means high-quality, large companies like Amazon, Johnson & Johnson, or Microsoft. But these stocks got their name from the chips or tokens used by 19th-century gamblers, with blue being the highest value. Make what you like of the fact that the kind of stock recommended for "widows and orphans" takes its name from a poker game!

Oddly enough, there's no official list of the Nifty Fifty; there might have actually been fifty-one or fifty-two. These included a lot of household names, such as Coca-Cola, American Express, Procter & Gamble, Avon, JC Penney, Gillette, Eastman Kodak, IBM, and McDonald's. Of course, the fact that you've heard of the company behind the stock gives you a feeling that you understand exactly what it does. Coca-Cola makes soft drinks, IBM is in computing, and the Avon lady coming to call will bring the cosmetics company right into your home. This made investors feel even safer.

Originally, investing in these stocks was a reasonable investment idea. Stable companies with higher than average growth, a high market share, and well-regarded products are definitely worth investing in. However, the problem was the increasingly high prices being paid for these stocks. Over the long term, American stocks have traded around fifteen to sixteen times earnings—that is, it would take fifteen years at this year's level of earnings to repay the share price. But the Nifty Fifty traded at fifty times earnings or more by the early 1970s—far too high to be justifiable. Investors were buying on sentiment and ignoring valuations.

When the 1973–74 bear market began, the Nifty Fifty tumbled. In 1972, at the height of the Nifty Fifty, McDonald's was valued at fifty times earnings. The shares fell from $75 to $25, despite the fact that the business was still doing well and has continued to expand ever since. (Peter Lynch cites this as a classic example of overpaying for a good business.) Polaroid lost 90 percent of its value in 1973.

How would you have avoided losing your money in this disaster? It's fairly simple. If you learned how to value stocks, for example, by reading Benjamin Graham's The Intelligent Investor or another good book on securities valuation, you'd have seen that valuations were extremely high and that the future growth rate needed to make those valuations correct was also improbably high. Understanding that a stock has a value, as well as a price, would have meant that as prices went up, you would have been checking whether you needed to change your portfolio and look for less spectacularly valued shares.

A second lesson is that there is no such thing as "buy and hold forever." You may be a less active and more patient investor, and you may have an average holding period of years, but if a stock becomes too expensive or if sudden bad news makes your original investment assumptions untenable, then you need to sell.

(As a side note, the Nifty Fifty is also one of India's main stock market indices, but it has nothing to do with the American version.)

The worst thing about the Nifty Fifty bubble and collapse is that many of the investors buying those shares believed they were making a risk-averse investment. Their financial advisors and the press encouraged them to believe that these household names and their solid business backing meant the people could not lose by buying shares. In fact, because of the high valuations, they were buying a ticking timebomb.

Eurotunnel/Eurostar/Getlink

Although the United Kingdom's economy is bound up with the European economy, it is separated from the continent by the English Channel. Until Eurotunnel was started, the only way of traveling from England to France was by air or on a ferry boat, despite the fact that on a good day, you could actually see the French coast from Dover. Eurotunnel proposed to put an end to Britain's isolation and create a fixed link between the two.

Eurotunnel was a joint operation between France and the UK, but it was a private enterprise. Its plans were to dig two parallel tunnels through which would run "shuttle" trains carrying cars and trucks between depots close to the coast and Eurostar trains between London and Paris for individual passengers.

Originally funded by corporate shareholders, many of them contractors who would be involved in the project, it issued shares to the general public in 1987, though it was not expected to open for business until 1993.

Unfortunately, the operations soon ran into trouble. For instance, one of the huge tunneling machines ran into a bad patch of ground, which hadn't been expected by geologists. Water got into its engine, and it needed to be written off and taken out of the way. The lack of clarity about who made decisions led to trains being ordered with six-hundred-millimeter doors. The French railway authorities demanded seven-hundred-millimeter instead, leading to delays and extensive rework and duplicated costs. This single change is said to have cost an amazing $70 million.

The shares were originally floated at £3.50. The first day was a disaster. The shares dropped to £2.50 by the close of trading. However, at their peak, the shares achieved a price of £7.99, which was not bad for a company with a nine-billion-euro debt and made no money at all. When the tunnel opened, both passenger projections and expected ticket prices turned out to be far off the mark. The business continued to make a loss for years.

Because of the costs, the company had huge bank debts and huge debt servicing payments to meet. Eventually, a reorganization of capital was required. The debt was renegotiated, but as a result, shareholders' stakes in the business were drastically diluted. That reorganization wasn't enough to plug the holes, so there was a second change in capital. Now, the banks controlled the company, and the shares were worth almost nothing. The first dividend wasn't paid to shareholders until 2009—twenty-two years after the fundraising.

The company changed its name to Getlink in 2017. It seemed set for a more promising future until the world event that started 2020. In 2021, following the lockdowns, Getlink had to be bailed out again.

Big engineering projects are always a risk, but not all have such huge problems. One reason that Eurostar had such a troublesome time executing the project was that the line between client and contractor was blurred. Contractors, such as Taylor Woodrow, Costain, Bouygues, and Spie-Batignolles, as participants in Trans-Manche Link (TML), owned part of the company alongside a number of major banks. They were, therefore, owners of the business and assessed and awarded the contracts for building the tunnel, which was a clear conflict of interest.

The project was originally expected to cost $7.5 billion. One and half billion dollars in equity were raised in 1987, together with $500,000 in private finance, for a project that would cost $7 billion even if it was delivered on time and on budget. Spending increased to $15 billion by 1994 and $23 billion by 1995, more than three times the expected level. By this time, the contractors were suing the company for additional payments, so legal costs were also being added to the bill.

The business plan depended on a number of crucial assumptions about the level of passenger and freight traffic that the tunnel would take on and about pricing. French railway operator SNCF's traffic figures proved far too optimistic. At the same time, when shuttle services opened, the company had to increase its prices above those of the ferry companies that competed with it on the Dover-Calais route in order to cover its costs. It did not gain a significant share of traffic; the ferries were actually able to increase their daily crossings significantly. The company was more successful with the London-Paris traffic, which competed largely with airlines.

Operations had a high fixed cost, so only operating at high-capacity utilization would make a profit. At the same time, paying interest on its massive debt prevented the company from making a profit. It was still not profitable in 2000.

What were the signs of trouble for Eurotunnel? First, the nature of the project as a dual national (UK-French) company with complex structuring and with contractors owning a share indicated this wasn't going to be smooth sailing. However, a 25 percent contingency was allowed in the original financing plan for cost overruns.

The bigger problem was that Eurotunnel had an apparent but not a real monopoly. Although it was the only fixed link across the Channel, it competed with both ferries and airlines. This leads to an interesting comparison with other engineering-based projects, such as solar farms or power stations. Most infrastructure businesses of this sort have an output agreement that specifies the minimum and maximum volumes and usually links prices to inflation. Eurotunnel was dependent on the open market.

However, if one invested at the beginning, there were plenty of opportunities to sell the stock at a profit or a minor loss once it became evident there would need to be a bailout. But why didn't investors do that? The main reason is they considered the project "too big to fail."

The Eurotunnel project would not fail, true. Both governments had a huge interest in ensuring the infrastructure was completed and entered use. And the banks surely did not want to write off their loans to the business. In this sense, it was indeed "too big to fail." Where investors made a bad mistake was in believing that this meant shareholders' money was safe. The project was saved but at their expense.

Russia

The phrase "too big to fail" was also bandied about a lot by fund managers and bankers talking about Russia in the 1990s as it left communism and started to develop a capitalist system.

Many things were wrong with Russia at a time when other Central and Eastern European countries (like Estonia, the Czech Republic, and Poland) were making fast progress. It should have kept many investors out. For instance, throughout the 1990s, the Russian economy actually shrank.

Most Russian companies had production facilities that were both old and old-fashioned, so their costs were high and their quality low compared to companies elsewhere. Many were still run in the traditional Soviet way, with only very basic accounting. They were more focused on volume, not profitability. The economy was still focused on commodities and heavy industry, and according to one IMF (International Monetary Fund) report, "Russia was in large part a virtual economy with large unrehabilitated industries producing negative value-added goods." Falling oil prices in 1996 and 1997 didn't help either.

Since companies had no way to evaluate returns, they frequently made poor investments. Few had globally competitive products. Many investors were interested in the military-industrial complex as a source of technology, but this, too, was way behind the West. Companies making spare parts often had only two customers: Israel (which still used Kalashnikovs) and Russia.

Elsewhere in Central and Eastern Europe, many businesses were sold to foreign companies. This introduced new working practices, expertise, and plants. However, this did not happen in Russia.

Add to this the fact that price controls still existed, which means companies were not free to set their prices. Many companies had a rate of return on assets that was significantly lower than the interest rate, and things did not look good. Russia had also failed to pass legislation protecting the rights of minority shareholders, and the legal system was a mess. There was no certainty that investors would be paid out in dividends, and they had no influence on company management.

However, "Russia is too big to ignore" became a mantra in the investment community. The RTS (Russian Trading System) index rocketed from less than one hundred in 1996 to just over five hundred in 1997 as investors bought stocks, such as dominant gas company Gazprom, telecoms provider Rostelekom, and gas producer Lukoil. The market was up 142 percent in 1996 and another 98 percent in 1997, making it the best performing emerging market for the period, despite the fact that its economy was continuing to contract. (This was at a time when Asian markets were collapsing like dominoes.)

Boris Yeltsin's reelection and his appointment of a government of young reformers were taken as good omens. In 1997, Euromoney magazine awarded Anatoly Chubais the title of world's best finance minister.

But investors had been bamboozled. Russia was certainly big, with a huge population and massive natural resources, but it wasn't profitable. Unlike other emerging markets, it didn't have a growing middle class; in fact, the middle class that already existed had seen its wealth disappear in devaluations and bank busts. Pensions and state wages were not being paid, which anyone could discover if they took a trip out of central Moscow and visited one of the smaller cities, as a few smart investment bankers did.

The numbers were all there to be seen. The problem was that investors were fooling themselves by looking at pretty projections rather than reality. As the extent of the problem became evident, many investors turned "too big to ignore" into "too big to fail," hoping the IMF or the World Bank would step in to save them.

In August 1998, Russia defaulted on its sovereign debt. The RTS ended the year 85 percent down.

A new politician took control afterward. One of the things he said at the time was, "To reach the production level of Portugal and Spain, two countries that are not known as leaders of the world economy, it will take Russia approximately fifteen years if the GDP grows by at least eight percent a year."

That shows how wrong the investment bankers were about Russia being "too big to ignore." But he did manage to start pushing things the right way, at least for a while.

His name, you might like to know, was Vladimir Putin.

Enron

Every deregulation creates winners. In London, the "Big Bang" broking changes of the mid-1980s let little broking firms become huge investment banks. In the US, President Obama's JOBS Act pretty much created the property crowdfunding market. And back in the late 1980s, the deregulation of the US energy market also created conditions that nimble firms like Enron were able to exploit, particularly once the internet got up and running in the late 1990s.

For instance, Enron created Enron Online (EOL), an electronic trading website through which companies could trade energy commodities. Fortune magazine was so impressed that it named Enron America's most innovative company for 1996, 1997, and every year until 2001. From 1998 to 2000, its stock more than doubled, going from $20 to $40, and then rose steeply to hit a high of just over $90.

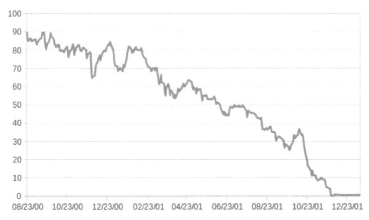

Enron's stock price from the summer of 2000 to early 2002.
User:Nehrams2020 (original), User:0xF8E8 (SVG), CC BY-SA 3.0
<*https://creativecommons.org/licenses/by-sa/3.0*>, via Wikimedia Commons;
https://commons.wikimedia.org/wiki/File:EnronStockPriceAugust2000toJanuary2001.svg

However, Enron's earnings were a sham. The company had used aggressive accounting practices together with special purpose vehicles (companies set up to hold debt and liabilities outside the parent company) to present a falsely attractive picture to investors. By the end of 2001, Enron was a penny stock, having fallen to just twelve cents.

One of the biggest issues was "mark to market" (MTM). This accounting practice is really intended for businesses like investment banks and traders. It measures the value of a security on the basis of the current market price rather than the historic cost. It's quite sensible for that type of business. However, it's not intended to work for long-term assets, such as power plants. Enron, on the other hand, happily adopted MTM for power plants, recording them in the books not at what they had cost to build but at the anticipated profit they would make.

If the assets didn't make the expected profit, though, they would have to be written off. But Enron dealt with that problem by transferring unprofitable assets to SPVs (special purpose vehicles, which companies set up to obtain deals), which didn't have to report figures and so could hide the loss. The SPVs also borrowed money on Enron's behalf so that the figures in the company's SEC filings showed a debt position much more favorable than was really the case.

Enron did quite a good job of hiding its weaknesses. However, Jim Chanos of Kynikos Associates, a well-known short seller, decided to take a position against the stock, which delivered him great returns. He had worked out that management was using overly optimistic accounting techniques. He also believed that Enron was not really making money. It had a return on capital of 7 percent, but he thought its cost of capital was as high as 9 percent; in other words, it was paying its banks and shareholders more than it could afford.

There aren't many things Jim Chanos doesn't know about finance. In fact, he lectures on the subject at Yale. He carried out in-depth work on Enron. But could you have worked out what was going on? In fact, just checking the cost of capital and the return on capital using publicly available data is quite easy to do and would have shown that there was a problem with the accounts.

Another big red flag was the increasing hostility of company management to analysts' and journalists' questions. On one conference call, CEO Jeffrey Skilling called analyst Richard Grubman "an asshole." Obviously, he was rattled. What was he afraid of? The answer became apparent not long afterward.

Enron Stock Price, 1997-2002

Source: Enron Securities Ligitation website

Enron stock price.

SPACs: The Bubble That's Just Unwinding

It's always worth asking whether there are any vested interests at work when you're looking at an investment. An example of vested interests is the believers. You might find them on social media or in the press; they're the people who have invested their own self-respect in a "pet" stock. The other set is more serious; they're the sponsors, the people who make money out of promoting a stock or advising a company.

For instance, if you found yourself back in 1720, before buying South Sea Company stock, if you had thought, "Why is the government supporting this company?" or "Why are all the politicians buying this stock?" then you might have realized the investment was intended to benefit the government rather than the investor.

In 2021, when a large number of SPACs (Special Purpose Acquisition Companies) were being issued, some observers noted the very favorable terms on which sponsors were rewarded. Sponsors provide the company's initial capital and are rewarded with a large stake in the company compared to their cash investment. A sponsor could make millions of dollars for just $25,000 cash up front. They are also incentivized to make an acquisition before the two-year cutoff point, at which time IPO (initial public offering) investors can ask for their $10 a share back.

With a little more research, you would find out that it would be quicker and cheaper for an owner or manager of a business to create a SPAC and then buy back their business rather than carrying out an IPO. You'd also find that one of the reasons for this is that SPACs aren't as tightly regulated and don't have to produce audited accounts, proper forecasts, and so on. That, again, is a warning sign. The benefits to sponsors are very clear, but the benefits to investors are less so.

Indeed, Michael Klausner and Michael Ohlrogge of Stanford and New York University calculated that for every $10 invested in the IPO by the time the average SPAC had made an acquisition, it only had $6.67 left. Investors had already lost over 30 percent of their investment, in effect subsidizing the business.

A few SPACs worked. Most did not.

Conclusion

All of these investment disasters sucked in investors' money and gave them nothing for it. Only one (Enron) was an outright crooked scheme; the others were honest investments that went bad.

The next investment disaster lying in wait for your money probably isn't quite the same as any of those you've read about in this chapter. But it's probably pretty similar. Akerlof and Shiller, in their book Phishing for Phools, say, "Yes, every time it's different—but, also, every time it is the same."

Recognizing types of risks and patterns of behavior and asking relevant questions will help save you from investment disasters of all types. Harry Markopoulos did a huge amount of detailed work on Bernie Madoff's investment business in order to arrive at his conclusion that Madoff was a fraud. He attempted to simulate

Madoff's returns and couldn't make the numbers add up. He was a professional fraud investigator; unfortunately, though he tipped off the SEC, the SEC decided to take no action.

But even without Markopoulos's advantages, you might have spotted a few problems with the investment.

Madoff refused to give details of his "top secret" trading strategy.

In 2001, seven years before Madoff's schemes exploded in the press, financial magazine Barron's published an article raising issues about his trading record.

Madoff refused to have his investments audited.

In 2003, Renaissance Technologies started to withdraw its investments in the fund because of concerns about its strategy.

Madoff was said to be managing $15 billion in funds, but volumes on the options market would have only supported a $750 million fund. His fund was bigger than the market in which it was trading.

People were being brought into the fund by social engineering by being told that friends, celebrities, or other members of their social circles had invested. A cachet of exclusivity was used to explain why the fund didn't publish proper investor information.

Several prominent Wall Street firms refused to do business with the fund.

No one understood how Madoff could consistently make higher returns than the market.

The biggest issue of all was that financial advisors who acted as feeder firms to Madoff were encouraging their clients to invest their whole wealth or a very substantial part of it into the fund. Diversification—putting your eggs in a number of different baskets—is a basic part of personal finance management. Never trust anybody who tells you to bet the bank on a single investment.

You don't need to be an expert to avoid the worst disasters. But you do need to do a little work. Keep abreast of the news, do some big-figure, back-of-the-envelope calculations, look at in-depth articles (like those on Seeking Alpha or in Barron's, rather than following TV programs aimed at boosting their audience to get more ads), and think about the different stakeholders and what they get out of the investment.

Chapter 3: The Great Depression of the 1930s

"Nobody knows the trouble I've seen / Nobody knows my sorrow..."

I: Crash

The Roaring Twenties was a time of national growth. New technologies, such as the radio and the automobile, as well as FW Taylor's standardization of work methods, made a huge impact. There was a housing boom, the Great Gatsby, the Jazz Age, short skirts, and high stock prices, making this an exciting time to live.

But this was also a time when there was little regulation of the stock market. Ramping up shares and "painting the tape" were common. Speculators would buy huge amounts of stock, then pay journalists and newsletter writers to promote them, selling when the price had risen to make a massive profit. Nowadays, that would be called insider trading, but back then, it was par for the course.

Until 1927, the rising stock market reflected a booming post-war economy. Corporations were increasing their profits, and they were paying higher dividends to their shareholders. The GDP (gross domestic product) was growing at nearly 9 percent a year. But in 1928, the market seemed to have gotten ahead of the real economy. In the late-20th-century tech boom, high valuations were justified because "it will be different this time" and because new technology was going to accelerate the pace of change.

The stock market also benefited from the fact that the US government had created a whole new population of investors during World War I. The issue of liberty bonds had been designed so that even Americans with very small amounts of wealth could invest in them; a quarter of the total population were bondholders. Brokerages were set up everywhere, even on cruise ships, and transaction costs headed south as telegrams and telephones made dealing much easier.

A new financial instrument had been created: the investment trust. This allowed investors to place their money in a managed diverse fund. The market exploded. There were only 40 investment trusts in 1921; by 1929, there were 750. But new funds were often priced at a premium, and people often borrowed large amounts so they could buy more shares, making them significantly higher risk than many purchasers thought. Some funds had eight times more debt than equity. It wouldn't take much more than a 10 percent fall in the market to capsize the entire trust.

Worse, some trusts geared up by creating structures of nested investment trusts like a Russian doll. These made more money for their sponsors than they did for their investors.

Charles Ponzi, who was not a trust manager but the creator of an investment scheme that bought discounted postal reply coupons, was one of these fraudulent sponsors. He promised huge dividends from his fund but spent the money on his own luxurious lifestyle. He paid those investors who asked for a dividend out of the money subscribed by more recent investors, not out of his income. Most investors were happy with the share price and didn't ask for dividends. Instead, they let their money ride. The scheme collapsed a year later, and investors lost over $20 million. Such pyramid schemes have been known as "Ponzi schemes" ever since.

The housing boom led to a huge speculative boom in Florida. People weren't buying houses; they were buying housing land at 10 percent down and, in many cases, reselling them within the month so they didn't have to pay the next 25 percent of the purchase price.

And this was all fueled by low-interest rates. The Fed (Federal Reserve System) was terrified of stalling the economy by putting rates too high (it had gotten its fingers burned with a rate rise in

1920 that slowed the economy markedly). So, rates stayed low, while credit was easy to get. Stock speculators could easily borrow "call money" to trade on margin. (Call money is short-term finance repayable on demand.) By 1928, the Fed had lost control. Its rates were so low that you could borrow from a Fed bank and lend call money at 10 percent to make a huge profit. Nowadays, that would be called shadow banking.

This all came to an end in 1929. Volatility had been increasing for some time, with a huge rally with Herbert Hoover's election, but there were also major corrections that could almost be seen as "rehearsal" crashes. Then, in the fall, the big crash came.

It didn't take much. Roger Babson was practically the "little boy who cried wolf," as he'd been predicting a bear market since 1927, and the market had just kept going up. But when he made a speech in September 1929, people suddenly listened. It created a huge panic, and the New York Stock Exchange began to slide.

Funds that had too much debt were forced to sell shares. Investors who had bought on margin (only putting down a percentage of the share price) had to find funds to pay their brokers or sell their shares as brokers sent out margin calls. Investment trusts suddenly fell to a discount. Liquidity evaporated, as there were no buyers left that investors could sell to. The market was in a death spiral.

There was no liquidity in real estate either. Families who had bought houses they couldn't afford to keep found that they couldn't sell them.

The stock market continued to fall. It fell another 34 percent in 1931, halved in 1932, and fell a further 23 percent in 1933. It took until the 1950s to get back to 1929 levels.

II: Depression

A stock market crash doesn't always accompany a real estate crash. This time, it did. And the two crashes together were so severe that they impacted the economy. Consumer spending collapsed. The stock market and real estate boom had depended on a credit boom, but now, banks were finding that customers couldn't repay their debts. Lending stalled, and monetary tightening led to lower demand and eventually to deflation and a recession. In 1930, the

GDP of the US fell by 11.9 percent. (By contrast, 2020 saw just a 3.5 percent fall in GDP, despite the 2020 world event that disrupted industry and commerce.)

Some major public banks failed, producing panic and runs on banks, which is where depositors try to take out their money all at once. The Fed did nothing to save them. Individuals had no confidence that their deposits were safe. Businesses couldn't borrow, and since they couldn't borrow, they couldn't invest. This tightening of credit turned what might have been a short-term recession into a longer, deeper depression.

One way out would have been for the Fed to cut interest rates and flood the market with credit. This would have boosted consumption, but it would have undermined how the dollar was fixed (pegged) to gold. The rigidity of the gold standard made the Great Depression worse. The Great Depression was global, but Germany (which had been hit hard by the need to pay reparations for the First World War) and the US performed worse than many other countries. In the US, unemployment rose to more than 20 percent, and the construction sector practically came to a stop.

Unemployed men during the Great Depression.

The beginning of the upturn came with Franklin Delano Roosevelt's election in 1932. His campaign was based on his determination to use a big spending program to create jobs, infrastructure, and welfare. Up until then, conventional economics had insisted that the patient needed to be starved—that the credit cycle needed to end in a great purging. Instead, Roosevelt planned his New Deal to kick-start the economy with public spending.

It was called the New Deal, but it was actually a plethora of different programs and plans. Not all of them worked. Some were quietly dropped, while others were beefed up, operating pragmatically on the basis of finding out what worked. It wasn't ideologically based, and it worked at the grassroots as well as in Washington. And it worked. Beginning in 1933, the US set itself back on the path toward growth, though the New Deal was never quite big enough to make the nation prosperous. (Roosevelt was handicapped by his desire to try to square the circle, balancing the budget at the same time as financing the New Deal.)

III - Who Made Money?

Some people still managed to make money throughout the 1929 crash and the Great Depression. It's interesting to look at the list, as it gives an idea of several ways that you might approach poor economic conditions should they occur in the future.

Irving Kahn started his career as a broker in 1928, and his first trade was a short sale the next year. (A short sale is when an investor sells without having the stock so that he can buy it later at a lower price. It is a high-risk transaction, but if the market is in free fall, short sellers can make a lot of money.) Kahn continued shorting the market. He doubled his money in the crash, founded his own fund management business, and lived to be 109. It's worth noting that he was a disciple of Benjamin Graham, "the father of value investing," so he had a clear idea in mind of what was a reasonable value for a stock. He sold because he believed the stocks he was looking at were extremely overvalued. He was not speculating but relying on his calculations of what businesses were really worth.

Shorting is risky. If the market had turned around, Kahn would have had to close his short positions and could have lost his money. But in those conditions, it worked.

Jesse Lauriston Livermore was another "short seller" and is said to have made $100 million from short selling during the crash. He's not a role model like Kahn, though. Livermore had already been broke once, and apparently, he managed to lose the money he'd made in rather short order. He committed suicide in 1940 after becoming bankrupt again.

So, short trading is not automatically a get-out clause in a down market. Kahn kept what he made, but Livermore handed it all back.

Some investors actually exited the market gradually during the final years of the Roaring Twenties. **Bernard Baruch**, for instance, had done well in the early 1920s bull market, but he started selling short in 1927 and 1928 and refused to join the pool of financiers who bought back stocks to try to revive the market. Like Kahn, he appears to have taken his view on valuation grounds.

Joseph Kennedy was already wealthy, with experience in banking and stockbroking, as well as real estate investing. He had taken advantage of the boom—he'd been behind a couple of share-ramping operations—but he knew that the boom was on its last legs and liquidated his stock market investments. After the crash, he developed real estate instead. He actually grew his wealth during the Great Depression from $4 million in 1929 to $180 million in 1935.

John Maynard Keynes, a British economist, lost 80 percent of his fortune in the initial crash. But in 1933, he went back into the market and bought preference shares in US utilities, which had been beaten down because of worries about government regulation. (Preference shares pay a fixed dividend, and the dividend has to be paid before other shareholders get anything.) Keynes tripled his money on that one series of trades.

What did Keynes get right? First of all, although he stayed in the market too long, he was quick to realize that things had changed. He was one of the earliest commentators to spot that the situation had moved from a pure stock market crash to a major economic downturn. Secondly, he was focused on finding a bargain. He bought his preference shares at a vast discount to their true value and was confident enough to defy the conventional wisdom and make a contrarian buy.

Outside the stock market, a few far-sighted individuals made their fortunes during the Depression by focusing on what an impoverished America needed. **Michael Cullen** built up King Cullen Groceries to provide cheaper basic goods to American families. The self-service stores had large selections of goods at discount prices. Cullen had, in effect, invented the supermarket.

Chrysler used the Depression years to steal second place in the auto market from Ford. The reason how was quite simple; it focused on making cheaper cars. In the 1920s, it was a bit player, but by 1933, it had a quarter of the market.

Two men made their fortunes by investing in bargain shares in the aftermath of the crash. **John Templeton** invested $10,000 in shares once they hit multi-year lows, finding stocks he felt offered value for the future. By the 1940s, they had quadrupled in value, and Templeton founded a major fund management business. **J. Paul Getty**, meanwhile, was fortunate enough to inherit $500,000 in 1930, which he put to work, grabbing bargain-basement oil stocks. By the 1950s, he had become America's richest man.

So, remember that a stock market crash always creates opportunity, as does a recession. But you need to be careful about how you use that opportunity, and you also need to be careful about how you finance your investments. You want to have a margin of error and can wait things out if you are a bit ahead of the market.

John Dillinger's name should perhaps be added to the list of people who made money during the Great Depression. He did so by the simplest of means: go where the money is, and steal it. That is, he robbed banks. However, his example probably should not be followed. First, it's unethical. And secondly, the FBI caught up with him in 1934 and shot him dead.

15 ways to future-proof yourself

1. Make sure you have an emergency fund. Ideally, it should represent at least three months of living expenses or, even better, six. Don't take any risks with this money.

2. Don't overcommit your budget. If you are not able to save any of your monthly paycheck, you have a problem. You either need to make more money or spend less.

3. Be ready to buy cheap. It's always worth having some cash in reserve so that if the market falls, you can take advantage of the bargains that present themselves. Those might be stocks, duplexes for renting out, or a family business that you can take over and turn around.

4. Don't overleverage. If you have too much debt, try to pay it down as fast as you can. Pay the expensive debt and debt that's repayable on demand (like overdraft) first.

5. Watch out for high leverage in the markets. If corporations are highly indebted, if lenders are financing 100 percent mortgages, or if households are taking on massive amounts of credit card debt, it's a sign that the economy and the stock market could be overheating. Get in the habit of checking official statistics for these numbers.

6. Be careful of exuberance. All kinds of bling, crazy spending, or trophy acquisitions by major corporations are all signs that things could be getting out of hand. If you see a newspaper that's targeted to working-class people advertising $600 dresses and $50,000 kitchens, something is wrong. It may not be a sign the market will fall the next week, but it's still a concern.

7. If the market crashes, be ready to get out fast while you can unless you are prepared to wait things out. Liquidity (the ability to sell) is always an issue, but in the first few days, it's usually possible to sell. Focus on getting out of the stocks that are the most highly valued, those about which you had concerns, and those that will be challenged to respond to new market conditions (e.g., if interest rates are going up, sell those with high debts).

8. Keep an eye on valuations. While Baruch spotted that valuations were too high and got rich by gradually exiting the market before the crash, Getty, Keynes, and Templeton saw where valuations were low and grabbed assets for a fraction of what they were worth.

9. Don't try to time the market exactly. You will never sell right at the top, and you will never buy right at the bottom. Every investor leaves some money on the table, even the best guys. At the same time, remember that it's not "all or

nothing." You can trim your stock market holdings without selling out completely, and you can reinvest on the way up piece by piece.

10. Anticipate contagion. If one market falls—whether that's commodities, the stock market, or the housing market—then it's likely to affect others. Think through the ways that things are likely to play out, and make your bets accordingly.

11. Don't believe the government will stop the market from falling, or the banks will stop the market from falling, or the Stock Exchange will sort things out. In fact, when NYSE Vice President Richard Whitney walked out on the floor of the stock exchange and started buying blue chip stocks, that would have been a really excellent time to sell. Markets have a rhythm of their own, and no one tells them what to do.

12. Diversify your holdings. That includes having savings in two different banks in case the worst happens.

13. In a depression, whether you're investing in your own business or in stocks, look for ways to help people and businesses cut their costs and meet their budgets. Invest in low-cost suppliers and companies that supply basic goods.

14. Don't rob banks.

15. Try to help other people if you can by displaying solidarity and empathy. The New Deal worked because it engaged ordinary Americans in making their country better in a tangible way. Get engaged, and get active.

Can we see parallels with the depression today? Some features of society and the recent economy are similar to what we saw in the Roaring Twenties: increasing inequality, conspicuous consumption by the wealthy, and a stock market that has been on a major bull run and looks highly valued. And we already had a crash and recession in 2008 that looked a bit like the "rehearsal" crashes in the mid-1920s.

However, one big difference at the moment is that there's not a New Deal. Instead, central banks globally decided on a program of quantitative easing. They decided to support the markets by buying bonds. This actually increased inequality since it increased asset prices. People who owned shares, houses, and rental properties saw their wealth increase at the expense of those who didn't hold assets (renters and workers).

In 2020 and 2021, the US and Europe have generally decided to support businesses and households with funding in a way that's reminiscent of the New Deal. However, spending so far has focused on saving the economy from collapsing rather than investing in new infrastructure or investment in technology and industry. The jury is out on whether it's going to be enough.

Perhaps taking a look at the 2008 crash and economic crisis and the reaction to it will help to assess where things are likely to head in the next decade.

Chapter 4: The Great Recession of 2008

"Booms go boom." -Fred Schwed - *Where are the Customers' Yachts?*

The subprime mortgage crisis of 2007 came like a bolt from the blue. The housing market in the US had been doing well. The price of the average American house more than doubled between 1997 and 2006. The stock market was also doing well, having recovered from the tech crash.

While stock markets are often said to "climb a wall of worry," continual increases in housing prices never seem to worry homeowners. They are only of concern to those who are priced out of the market. And since subprime loans at keen prices were available even to the less creditworthy, most Americans could afford to buy. With housing prices going up, homeowners believed they were making money every day, and banks believed they would easily be repaid for the risks they were taking.

Housing booms and busts have happened before. What was different with this one was that a new way of financing mortgages had been created: mortgage securitization. Instead of a bank lending its own money (or rather, its depositors' money) to homeowners, the bank would package a number of mortgages together and sell it as a security to investors as an MBS (mortgage-backed security) or CDO (collateralized debt obligation). The investors, in effect, were buying the interest payments and eventual repayment on the mortgage. The bank, meanwhile, was making a profit on the transaction. Credit default swaps (CDS), a form of insurance against default, also helped to deliver risk-free income streams to investors.

Americans had to spend more to acquire a home, which led to vastly increased levels of personal debt. From 1980 to 2001, the ratio of median home prices to median annual household income was around 3 times; by 2006, it had hit 4.6 times. Meanwhile, US household debt as a percentage of annual disposable income had hit 127 percent by 2007 compared to just 77 percent in 1990. In other words, Americans would have had to work for a year and three months just to pay off their debt, even in a tax-free world.

The US housing market peaked in 2006. Defaults and foreclosures increased, as they always do at the end of a housing boom. However, this time, other factors were at play too. Investor demand for MBSs collapsed, and by July, investment bank Bear Stearns's two MBS funds had imploded. Bear Stearns had to be rescued by the Fed. Later, the US government's two housing loan organizations, Fannie Mae and Freddie Mac, had to be bailed out, as did AIG, the insurer that had issued credit default swaps on a huge number of MBSs. (If AIG went down, banks would have fallen like dominoes.) Lehman Brothers, on the other hand, was allowed to fail since the Fed considered it not big enough to pose a systemic risk to the banking system.

The result of the subprime crash was a full-scale recession, not just in the US but also globally. It took until 2014 for the US to get GDP per capita back to 2007 capitals; the UK and Spain took even longer. In Europe, there was a knock-on effect on banks and sovereign debt, with many peripheral countries needing support from the European Central Bank.

In 2008/9, the unemployment rate in the US doubled from 5 percent to 10 percent. (There was a huge spike to 14.7 percent in April 2020, but this has now corrected itself and was due to a non-economic shock, not to underlying economic reasons.)

There were a few people who realized that one or two aspects of the boom were unsustainable. Fund manager Steve Eisman, investor Michael Burry, and the staff at Cornwall Capital all correctly diagnosed the problems with the MBS market and were able to make money by shorting it. Meredith Whitney, a banking analyst at Oppenheimer, predicted the banking crisis and, in particular, the collapse of Bear Stearns and Citigroup.

These analysts and fund managers relied on their own detailed investigation of the loan terms being made and the quality of the MBS packages being sold. That probably isn't something most private investors would be able to do; it takes not only specialized knowledge but also a lot of time and access to detailed documentation.

However, some observers of the housing market were also worried about the sustainability of the boom, not just in the US. Mortgage defaults were already rising in the US in 2006, giving a clear signal to those who listened.

Some other countries were very severely impacted. Spain saw a huge boom in construction, building five million new dwellings between 2001 and 2008. That was more than both Germany and France combined, even though the Spanish population was (and still is) much smaller than the population of the other two countries. Most of these dwellings were targeted at foreign buyers of holiday homes; very few of them were in the main cities, where most of the population lived. Most of them were also built by developers who had borrowed significant amounts from the banks and depended on the sales of apartments to repay their debts.

Spain was left with ghost developments that were never finished, a construction sector that had practically collapsed, and a major banking crisis.

Real estate agents, of course, didn't have a problem repeating the bullish mantras of "sun, sea, sand will never go out of fashion" and "invest on the ground floor," even while prices were headed downward.

In Ireland, economic growth since the 1990s had been rapid. But from 2003 onward, while the economy continued to be strong, debt was rising fast, and higher mortgage debt fed into sharp rises in housing prices. In late 2000, the IMF published a report that said Irish property prices had risen too fast, predicting a crash in the medium term. The Irish government poured petrol on the fire by adding tax incentives for both owner occupiers and landlords into the mix. Credit expansion accelerated sharply, with developers borrowing to finance new housing on a grand scale, as well as household borrowing. By 2012, houses were selling for half the prices they'd achieved in 2007.

Clongriffin, an Irish "ghost town."
William Murphy, https://www.flickr.com/photos/infomatique/24460799536; https://creativecommons.org/licenses/by-sa/2.0/

One problem was the "boy who cried wolf" syndrome. All the way from 2000 onward, the IMF, the Economist magazine, the Central Bank, and the Economic and Social Research Institute said on numerous occasions that Irish property was overvalued. But the market hadn't crashed in 2001; it kept trending upward. That deprived these commentators of credibility, although they were, in fact, right.

In this case, you could have seen the pieces. You could have tracked the increasing debt per household. You could have also noticed that yields on renting out property had fallen below the interest rate on government bonds. In other words, you could put money in a risk-free investment and earn more than you did with a house that needed to be actively managed, insured, and maintained and where void periods or bad tenants represented a significant risk.

In the UK, the housing market kept heading upward. What signs might you have seen there? The availability of mortgages that lent more than the price of the property was definitely a sign of credit having become too loose. Banks generally rely on the buyer's deposit of 10 percent (or more) to give them security, as they would know that the loan is more than covered by collateral. If the borrower "walks," the bank can sell the house for 10 percent below the original valuation and still make the books balance. With a 100 percent or more mortgage, there's no such margin of error. With Northern Rock's "Together" mortgage, at a 125 percent loan to value ratio, there was no margin of error at all.

The house price to income ratio had also been rising fast. Generally, it had stayed around three to four times for most of the 1990s, but by 2004, it had risen to six times and to eight times in London.

So, it perhaps wasn't surprising that when housing prices fell, they fell fast. UK prices were down 15 percent in 2008, according to Nationwide Building Society. What's more surprising is that the UK housing market promptly recovered. Because there was no building boom, there was no excess supply of unsold property to be soaked up. The Bank of England's response to the crisis was to keep interest rates low, and though liquidity was tight for a time, lending soon resumed. Fast forward to 2021, and the housing price income ratio had hit seven times, despite stagnating incomes, economic decline, the major world event of 2020/2021, and the immense disruption of Brexit. In London, where foreign buyers were prominent, it stood at eleven times.

Would you buy a house in Britain at the moment?

While 2008 didn't happen in quite the same way as 1929, there are some definite similarities. Low-interest rates, low returns on most financial investments, and the hunt for yields are all similarities between the Roaring Twenties and the "Roaring 2000s." The creation of new financial instruments is also similar. In the case of the 1920s, it was investment trusts, and in the case of 2000, it was MBSs, CDOs, 100-percent-plus loan-to-value (LTV) mortgages, and interest-only mortgages.

The huge expansion of credit was also a link between most countries that had severe problems in 2008. In France, where the amount that could be lent to individuals was controlled by law so that banks were unable to loosen their credit requirements, the impact was much less severe. The problems of French banks were mainly related to the fact that many of them had invested in sovereign or bank debt from less prudent countries, such as Spain. (This shows that though France avoided a housing market crash, it didn't completely avoid contagion.)

If you had seen the signs, there are a number of things you could have done. As a private investor, you probably could not have shorted the market. Those instruments available to private investors, such as covered warrants, have a very limited life. You could have lost your investment if they ran out just two days before the crash.

But you could have rebalanced your portfolio away from housebuilders, REITs (real estate investment trusts), and banks. You could have bought other sectors, such as basic household goods. If you had debt, you could have paid it off. Some people downsized their homes during the boom times, ensuring that when prices fell, they were less exposed. You might not have been able to make much money out of the bust, but you could have protected yourself quite well against its results.

Dave Ramsey's "Seven Baby Steps" outlines a basic plan for protecting yourself against a recession. If you can't tick at least the first three off your list, you shouldn't be investing in the stock market.

1. Save for your emergency fund. Dave Ramsey suggests $1,000. Do this before you do anything else.

2. Pay off all your debt (except the house). I have a slightly different approach than Dave. He says to pay off the smallest debt first. I think you're better off paying the most expensive debt.

3. Save six months of living expenses in an emergency fund.

4. Once you have your finances on an even keel, invest 15 percent for retirement. It doesn't need to be in a pension plan, but it does need to be invested in a sensible way, say in a mix of treasury bills, a set of global ETFs, and a bunch of REITs. (Exchange-traded funds give you low-cost access to a diversified base of equities, while REITs invest in real estate and pay you dividends out of the rent.) Try to find tax-efficient ways to invest, such as a Roth IRA or 401(k).

5.If you have kids, save for their college funds.

6.Pay off your home loan early. The earlier you pay, the less interest you'll pay on your debt. And owning your home free of all debt gives you immense freedom.

7.Keep building wealth, and give some away too!

While you may not feel particularly attracted to the FIRE movement (Financial Independence, Retire Early), it is well worth reading about. Take a look at some of the prominent blogs on the subject, like Mr. Money Mustache, Financial Samurai, or Chief Mom Officer. Most of the leading practitioners have given a good deal of thought to ensuring they can sleep at night no matter what the stock market does.

But the single most important thing you must do is to get that emergency fund together. You never know when you are going to need it. And the fact that we had a crash in 2008 doesn't mean there might not be another one around the corner.

Chapter 5: War and What It Does to the Market: A Violent Cycle

"War does not determine who is right - only who is left." -Bertrand Russell

There's a wonderful anecdote about the redoubtable Nathan Rothschild, head of Rothschild Bank in London. Knowing that the future of Europe was at stake, he rode out to be present at the Battle of Waterloo. As soon as the result of the battle was known, he made his way back to London to buy everything he could on the stock exchange before the rest of the city found out about Wellington's victory over Napoleon.

It's just a pity that it's (probably) not true.

Where Rothschild actually made his money was in financing the Duke of Wellington's army. He was commissioned by the British government to supply Wellington with the necessary funds. This opened the way for more business with the government. The business was highly lucrative and helped establish the recently founded bank as a major financial house.

Rothschild is also credited with the saying, "Buy when you see blood in the streets." (Investor John Templeton put it slightly more abstractly when he said, "Invest at the point of maximum pessimism.")

Let's see whether that's always been a sensible idea.

* * *

Barton Biggs, an investment strategist at Morgan Stanley, studied the way stock markets responded to the Second World War. He noted that "at least once in every century there has been an episode of great wealth destruction," so it's a more common occurrence than you might think.

He was quite surprised that stock markets seemed to know exactly when a turning point had come in the war. The "wisdom of crowds" seems to have worked exceptionally well in this case. But, of course, the big problem with trying to negotiate the stock market in a war is what happens if either your country's stock market or its currency gets destroyed.

For instance, in 1917, Vladimir Lenin nationalized the banks, abolished private property, defaulted on Russia's bonds, and closed the stock market down for good. Diversifying your investments within Russia wouldn't have helped you. Equities, bonds, real estate—you'd have lost the lot. (Technically, of course, this was a revolution, not a war.) There's an academic study by Philippe Jorion and William Goetzmann that has some horrifying statistics on global stock markets. Out of the thirty-nine they looked at, only five—the US, the UK, Canada, New Zealand, and Sweden—had traded without a break since 1920. Most had at least a short-term closure or "controlled" trading, while a large number had a longer interruption of trading. Eleven—over a quarter—were dead; the markets had closed and never reopened.

Another interesting stock market movement that Barton Biggs mentioned was the Japanese response to the North Korean attack on South Korea in 1950. Though the market plummeted at first, it quickly rose as investors realized how supplying the US Army's procurement needs would boost the still-recovering Japanese economy. In fact, from 1949 to 1989, the Nikkei 225 had a massive bull run.

During War

Many things happen during a war. Generally, they lead to wealth destruction for many people on both sides. For instance, there may be supply shocks since a war disrupts supply routes (as is happening now to oil, gas, and wheat due to the situation in Ukraine). The consequent rise in the price of energy hits many households hard. In the Second World War, the UK saw its standard of living sharply impacted by the fact that German U-boats made sea trade with the colonies difficult and dangerous. Transatlantic trade was also affected. In the US, silk stockings were no longer available since silk imports from Japan had ceased when the hostilities began. Nylon replaced them. But by 1942, nylon was being used in the war effort to make parachutes, ropes, and other equipment, so stockings of any kind were nearly impossible to get hold of. Black marketeers made thousands of dollars from the "grey" stocking market, which is an example of wealth creation during wartime but not necessarily one that you ought to follow.

If your country is involved in the war but is not directly being fought over, you're lucky. This was America's position in WWII. You can invest in the stock market or commodities markets safely. However, it's very different if your own country is being fought over. In that case, all your assets are at risk.

The expropriation of property is common, and generally, the largest and most prestigious properties are taken first. For instance, in WWII, a lot of French châteaux became German headquarters, and hotels were taken over for troop accommodations. During an occupation, looters target whatever is mobile and of value, such as paintings, antique furniture, fur coats, and even toilets and washing machines.

Government bonds, normally considered one of the safest investments, become one of the riskiest. During the US Civil War, the Confederacy issued bonds, notes, and paper money to support the war effort; the first tranche offered to repay six months after the secession treaty was signed, but later issues extended that to two years (perhaps a sign of the way the war was going). Before the end of the war, runaway inflation had reduced the value of the dollar. In late 1864, a Confederate dollar was worth only three US cents.

Of course, once the Union won the war, Confederate money and bonds became worthless. They were backed by a government that no longer existed.

Confederate $100 bill.
https://commons.wikimedia.org/wiki/File:Confederate_currency_$100_John_Calhoun.jpg

War can also leave a country in a state of general lawlessness. That has happened, for instance, in Syria and Iraq. When you see that kind of thing happening, you need to get out fast.

How Do You Know War Is Coming?

War usually takes people by surprise. For instance, even though Vladimir Putin was amassing Russian troops on the border of Ukraine in the first two months of 2022, his actual invasion on February 24th came as a surprise to many. (Barton Biggs would have been glad to know that the market had done a good job of anticipating the invasion.)

But there are a number of factors that indicate trouble is on the way, and not all of them are military-related.

As Ray Dalio says, "Before there is a shooting war, there is usually an economic war." Hyperinflation and unemployment were factors that allowed Hitler to come to power; the fact that Germany was paying huge reparations for the First World War led the country to have a particular hatred of the winners (the UK, the US, and France).

The US Civil War is another example. One of the major factors that made the war possible—the tinder that allowed the fire to get started—was the economic divergence between the North and South. The North was becoming an increasingly manufacturing-focused, value-added economy. The South remained an agricultural commodity economy, producing mainly tobacco and cotton, a trade that depended on low- or no-cost labor (slavery). It's simplistic to say that this was the cause of the war, but it was certainly a major factor.

Economic conflict can fester for a long time. On the other hand, an economic shock can act as the spark that makes it flare up. For instance, sudden high inflation or default on debt can turn grumbling into revolt or a cold war into a "hot" war.

Increasing inequality in a country, particularly in an entire region, can also lead to wars. Populist leaders will often respond to poverty and the lack of opportunities by pointing at "enemies" as the ones responsible. This kind of rhetoric will not always cause a war, but it is a key factor. It may also forecast moves against ethnic groups or minorities in the country who are held culpable for the state of affairs. In history, we can see this happening to Jews in Hitler's Germany, East Asians in Idi Amin's Uganda, or Chinese communities in Indonesia under Sukarno.

Such issues can slumber for years, but more often, a gradual deterioration occurs. For instance, in Germany, laws depriving Jews of the ability to work in certain sectors, own businesses, and so on were passed long before Kristallnacht and the beginning of the extermination program. Many Jews decided to emigrate early on; it was easiest for those who had established careers or wealth. Conductors Bruno Walter and Otto Klemperer made their way to the US, and the American film industry wouldn't be the same without Billy Wilder.

The earlier emigrants managed to take a good deal of their wealth with them. Afterward, it became more difficult, as capital controls and emigration taxes were introduced. The Warburg family emigrated in 1938 and helped save other Jewish lives, but to do so, they had to sell a bank with a book value of nearly 12 million Deutschmarks for 3.4 million. After they had paid the different fees and taxes, they were left with just 155,000 Deutschmarks.

Obviously, it pays to get out early.

Aftermath: Wealth Creation or Destruction?

While war almost always destroys wealth, the aftermath of war can be very different depending on the circumstances.

We have already looked at the South Sea Bubble and the Mississippi Company as ways governments tried to deal with the aftermath of wars. Both France and England ended the wars with high government debts, so reducing the government's interest payments became a priority. In the case of the South Sea Bubble, there was relatively little long-term impact. In the case of the Mississippi Company, the devaluation of currency and the French distrust of paper money and joint stock companies had a longer-term effect. (To this day, only 3 percent of the French own shares compared to 58 percent in the US.)

The two world wars had very different aftermaths. After the First World War, Germany was forced by the onerous provisions of the Treaty of Versailles to pay reparations to the Allies. These amounted to 80 percent of Germany's gross domestic product, putting a huge strain on the country's finances. This made the depression of the 1930s much worse in Germany than elsewhere and led to the increasing polarization of German politics between Nazis and communists. (John Maynard Keynes protested at the time, foreseeing what was likely to happen.)

Protectionism in the 1930s, such as the Smoot-Hawley Tariff Act of 1930 that raised tariffs on imports to the US, also damaged global markets between the two world wars.

On the other hand, after the Second World War, the Marshall Plan was conceived to kickstart European economies, including Germany's. A lot of investment went to fixing infrastructure and buildings that had been damaged in the war, but German industry also received a boost. Technical assistance to increase industrial productivity was also provided.

The Marshall Plan, though funded by the US, brought advantages to the US economy. European countries started to buy US goods, and the dollar started to be used as a reserve currency. The plan also boosted America's soft power (an approach where you cooperate instead of use outright force) in Europe.

At the same time, the beginning of European integration was happening. In 1951, the Treaty of Paris founded the European Coal and Steel Community, which included France, Italy, Germany, and the Benelux countries. This eventually became the European Economic Community and then the European Union. When communist rule in Central and Eastern Europe ended, the European Union was strong enough to integrate some of the newly independent countries. That, perhaps, was the real end of the Second World War, as Europe reintegrated the countries that Stalin had demanded as part of the peace treaty.

Ethnic Cleansing

One of the most horrifying aspects of the Second World War was the Shoah or Holocaust, Hitler's attempt to destroy the Jewish race. But Hitler is not the only leader to have persecuted a minority group. Louis XIV got rid of the Huguenots (French Protestants). Pol Pot got rid of the intellectuals. The wars in former Yugoslavia saw the massacre of more than eight thousand Bosniaks at Srebrenica. Idi Amin got rid of Asian shopkeepers and businesspeople. Ferdinand and Isabella of Spain expelled the Jews and Muslims (Mudejars). Even though they had confiscated the Jews' capital, they got rid of effective and educated administrators and financiers. The Muslims, likewise, had expertise in market gardening and building trades, particularly carpentry, which was difficult to replace.

Ethnic cleansing almost always impoverishes a country. Sometimes, other countries benefit. England did well at the expense of Spain and France by accepting Protestant refugees. Dutch Protestants brought new weaving technology with them, and Huguenots brought weavers, silversmiths, watchmakers, and horticulturalists. And Jewish scientists fleeing Germany increased the pace of innovation in the US. According to Stanford economist Petra Moser, the fields in which the Jews were most prominent saw a 31 percent increase in new patents.

Where Does That Leave Us Right Now?

With war currently being waged in Ukraine, this is an interesting time to write a chapter on war and the economy.

It is obvious that there is increasing polarization between the EU and NATO countries on one side and Russia and its few allies (Belarus and Iran) on the other. China has carefully refrained from taking a strong stance. The EU has taken on more joint responsibility than ever before. For instance, it gave Ukrainian refugees the right to live and work in any EU country and agreed to an EU-wide program of sanctions.

Russia is certainly trying to turn the clock back to pre-1989 and regain former USSR territories in the Caucasus, Central Asia, and the Baltic. However, Russian GDP per capita in 2021 was only a little higher than it was in 2008, and the economy remains reliant on commodity prices (particularly oil). The Russian population is lower than it was in the last century and is forecasted to fall further, unlike China or India.

It seems likely that Putin is making a high-stakes gamble because nothing else seems likely to break the stagnation that Russia is stuck in.

The two major economic interests in the world are China and the US, and this is probably where more danger of escalation lies, as the two countries' philosophies, politics, and ambitions differ greatly. The two compete for top place. China's economy leapfrogged the EU to second place in 2021 for the first time.

China now has 15 percent of global exports, while the UK's export share started falling at the beginning of the 20th century. America's export share has been falling for several decades now. China also has nearly two years of foreign exchange reserves, which gives it a very strong position. Unlike Russia, it has transformed its economy in the last twenty years. While a command economy isn't necessarily the best way to run a country, China has had the luxury of long-term planning. Deng Xiaoping evolved a seventy-year plan to double incomes back in 1978, and so far, it's working.

China also invests heavily in education; it currently puts out eight times more STEM graduates than the US. While US soft power remains high, China is increasing its investment in the Belt and Road initiative, making huge investments in Central Asia, Polynesia, and Latin America.

The big question is probably not whether Ukraine will win; it's who will dominate post-war reconstruction in Ukraine. Will it be the EU, the US, or China? Ultimately, it's not the result of a war that matters as much as the way the peace is agreed upon and what happens next. Wars are often no more than distractions in a much longer economic cycle.

What Can You Do?

"In the long run," as John Maynard Keynes said, "we are all dead." If a global nuclear war takes place, worrying about your investments is not going to be at the top of your mind. However, assuming the world manages to avoid that, it's sensible to think about potential threats to your wealth from international or civil wars.

One big lesson from the past is that you should never be too complacent. People often say, "Don't worry about that. They'll never let it happen." That kind of thinking is lazy, and it can have fatal consequences.

So, without being alarmist or joining the survivalists by buying guns, ammo, and a log cabin in the wilds, what can you do to maximize your chances of enjoying your wealth in the long term?

First of all, diversification is crucial. Families with a single asset, whether it's a hotel, a bank account, or shares in a business, are very vulnerable in disorderly times. Remember that it's no use diversifying in a single country; buy a property in another country (not part of the same political or economic bloc) or put liquid assets in a foreign-held account. Holding foreign currency, directly or through foreign assets, is a particularly good idea. For instance, having a Swiss franc or Japanese yen account is a good way to diversify away from the dollar. But most of these diversifications need a fair amount of capital. They are good for really wealthy people but perhaps not so much for the average family.

This is one reason why cryptocurrencies might be worth considering. They are not issued by a country, and your access to them is solely through your crypto wallet. In this context, buying a currency that has lower volatility is a good idea, so consider stablecoins based on material resources such as gold or ones that are backed by fiat currencies.

Secondly, don't buy bonds. Buy equities. Bonds in times of war lose their safe haven status and have a good chance of ending up worthless. They are also useless in times of high inflation. In many cases, equities have a major bull run after the end of hostilities.

Thirdly, consider some easily portable investments. If you had to cut and run tomorrow, what could you take with you? Jewelry, gold coins or ingots, and precious stones might be good choices. But keep the fact that you own them to yourself, and don't put them in a bank safe, as they could be easily confiscated by the newly constituted authority after an occupation.

And fourthly, as with stock markets, be willing to take a loss on your investments if you need to—it's better than losing your life.

Chapter 6: A Magic Formula? The Power of Hindsight

"To invest successfully over a lifetime does not require a stratospheric IQ, unusual business insights, or inside information. What's needed is a sound intellectual framework for making decisions and the ability to keep emotions from corroding that framework."-Warren Buffett

Some investors are well known as having been successful on a grand scale. For instance, most people have heard of Warren Buffett, "the sage of Omaha." Other investors are not as well known but have enjoyed great success nonetheless. This chapter will take a look at some notable investors and examine the methods and formulas that they used to beat the market. To end the chapter, we'll look at whether those methods are still useful today.

Ben Graham is known as "the father of value investing," and a number of well-known investors, such as Warren Buffett, John Templeton, and Joel Greenblatt, founded their own investing approaches on his teachings. Value investing consists of analyzing companies by looking at their business operations, annual reports, and financial ratios in order to establish what Graham called the company's intrinsic value. According to Graham, when you buy shares, you are not buying a stock but a share of a business. The value of the business rather than the stock price should guide your decisions.

Graham then developed the concept of a margin of safety. If you believe the shares are worth $50 based on your examination of the business, but you can buy them for $45, you have a $5 (or 10 percent) margin of safety. That covers you if you've been a bit optimistic about the business's future prospects. It also means that if you're right and the market eventually comes to recognize the true value of the business, you will make an 11 percent return on your $45 investment.

If there's one ratio that Graham really liked to use, it was the price-to-book value. This measures the number of the company's assets that theoretically "belong" to each share and compares this to the share price. For instance, if you bought a tenth of a block of flats that was worth $8 million for $400,000, you'd be buying at 0.5 price-to-book ($400,000 / $800,000). That would be a bargain. But if you paid $1 million for it, you'd be paying more than it was worth. The price-to-book would be $1,000,000 / $800,000, or 1.21. In other words, you'd have overpaid by 21 percent.

Warren Buffett was actually one of Ben Graham's students at Columbia University. He and Charlie Munger set up a business and have run the Berkshire Hathaway investment fund since 1970. While Buffett and Munger are value investors in the Ben Graham tradition, they had a slightly different way of running a business. For instance, they have invested in controlling stakes of companies and turned them around by putting in their own managers.

Buffett is a long-term investor by nature. He has said, "If you're not willing to own a stock for ten years, don't own it for ten minutes." He has owned Coca-Cola stock since 1988, believing that the 1987 market crash had left the stock undervalued. His fund now earns nearly $700 million a year in dividends from the investment.

He has gotten things wrong. First of all, he bought stakes in airlines just before the world event of 2020. Then, he bailed. If he had held on, he would have seen his shares in American Airlines double in a year. But at least he bit the bullet rather than letting things drift. Discipline is important, and if an investment isn't increasing value (for instance, you bought a turnaround company, but it doesn't turn around), then selling the investment to put the money to work somewhere else is usually the right decision.

One of the big ideas Buffett has popularized is that of a "moat" or defensive barrier—any competitive advantage that a business has that prevents others from competing with it on an equal basis. In the case of Coca-Cola, for instance, it's the brand value, together with a global network of bottling partners. In the case of some companies, it's access to low-cost materials, ownership of important locations, or patented technologies. For instance, an airline that has a high percentage of slots at major airports might be worth buying even if it's currently not profitable since those slots are assets other airlines don't possess. Looking for businesses with "moats" should rule out investments in the me-toos (a copy-cat business) and also-rans (a business that never becomes a leader), which are always the first to suffer in a downturn.

Warren Buffett likes to look at the P/E (price/earnings) ratio. This simply shows how many years it would take, at the company's current rate of profitability, to "pay off" your investment with earnings. If you were to buy a company at a P/E ratio of one, it would earn as much as you'd paid for it in a year. On the other hand, if you bought a company at a P/E ratio of fifty, either you'd have to wait fifty years, or the earnings would need to go up quite steeply. (If earnings doubled every year, by next year, you would have an effective P/E ratio of 25, and the year after that, a very reasonable 12.5.)

Peter Lynch is another famous investor. He began as an analyst for Merrill Lynch and was handed the failing Magellan Fund to see if he could put some pep into it. He turned it into one of the strongest performing funds in the US.

Lynch uses the same data as Ben Graham and Warren Buffett to analyze stocks. But he has two slight differences. Where Ben Graham was a pure value investor, always looking for a discount— that is, the margin of error—Lynch preferred to look for what he called "growth at a reasonable price" (GARP). So, he would invest in fast-growing companies even if they were trading at a higher valuation than the market if he believed in their management and their long-term growth prospects.

Lynch also puts a big emphasis on looking for ideas in the real world. For instance, he struck lucky several times with restaurant chains and franchises simply because he had noticed the concept at a local mall. He then researched the company intensively, including its cost base, its competition, and the room for the company to grow. If everything stacked up, he'd invest. He used his wife and daughters to give him input on fashion brands too.

Finally, Lynch talks a lot about being clear about what kind of investment you are making. He divides investments into different types: long-term growth, turnarounds, or cyclical investments like automakers. For instance, with auto companies, when the industry is in a downturn, he looks for secondhand prices to start moving upward. That's a sign that automakers aren't producing enough cars and that there's room for them to increase their margins by raising prices. The shares usually start performing soon after that. But because the business moves in big cycles, he will sell the shares again once the cycle has turned up. They're not a long-term holding.

On the other hand, long-term growth stocks, such as McDonald's, might stay in his portfolio pretty much forever.

One formula Lynch likes to use is the PEG or price/earnings to growth ratio. This goes a bit further than the P/E ratio and helps to put it in relation to the company's rate of growth. If you could buy either of two companies at twenty times earnings, you might want to look at the PEG ratio. For example, Company A is growing at 10 percent a year, while company B is growing at 25 percent a year. To get the PEG ratio, you simply divide the P/E ratio by the growth rate. Company A has a PEG ratio of 20/10=2. Company B has a PEG of 20/25=0.8.

Generally, if you buy at a PEG ratio of exactly one, you are buying a stock that is growing at just the right rate to justify its P/E ratio. If you have to pay more, you are paying extra for that growth. But if you can pay less than a PEG ratio of one, you are getting growth at a discount; the company is growing faster than it needs to justify the share price.

Buffett and Lynch are very well-known investors. Geraldine Weiss, "the dividend detective" or "Queen of Dividends," isn't as well known, but she should be. Like Buffett and Lynch, she was a follower of Benjamin Graham, but she used dividends rather than earnings as her main yardstick.

While the P/E ratio measures the earnings that theoretically "belong" to you as a shareholder, dividends are paid to shareholders in actual cash. For instance, if you hold Coca-Cola right now, you'll get paid forty-four cents for every share you hold every quarter. Some people get a lot of their income through dividends, so these can be important.

Weiss was obviously talented, but back in the 1960s, no one thought a woman could succeed as a stockbroker, and she couldn't find a job. So, instead, she decided to sell her ideas directly, founding the newsletter Investment Quality Trends. She signed her articles as "G. Weiss." It wasn't until 1977 that she felt confident enough to reveal that she was actually female. She wrote a fascinating book, Dividends Don't Lie, in 1988, and a follow-up, Dividends Still Don't Lie, was published by her successor at IQT, Kelley Wright, in 2010.

Weiss screened stocks on various criteria. First of all, stocks had to pay dividends. They also had to have a history of maintaining or raising the dividend. She looked for stocks with low debt, which meant that the dividend was safe, and she also considered standard value investor ratios, such as a P/E ratio of 20 or less and a price-to-book value of 2.0 or less.

Weiss did very well, right up to the 1990s. Then, suddenly, dividend stocks started to underperform as the technology sector boomed. Most tech stocks were young companies that didn't pay dividends even if they made profits; they preferred to reinvest in new capacities. However, she didn't change her approach. The technology crash showed that while things had gone against her for a while, the rules of the market hadn't changed.

All these investors were known for being active investors. They tried to pick the right investments and did a lot of research to try to get them right. They were trying to beat the market. Sometimes, it worked, and sometimes, it didn't, but it was a lot of work. If you invested in a mutual fund, you'd pay high charges for someone like Lynch to manage it. Then, Jack Bogle came along.

Bogle looked at mutual funds and immediately saw two things. One, they were expensive. Two, by definition, half of them would underperform, no matter how much you paid. His way of dealing with that was simple. Instead of trying to outperform the market, he would simply aim to match the market. He did that by buying every stock in the Dow Jones index.

That's a very simple way to invest. Because it doesn't need much managing, it's also a cheap way to invest. Eventually, Bogle's idea produced the exchange-traded fund (ETF), which has low costs and can be bought and sold on the stock exchange just like any other stock. An ETF won't outperform the market, but unlike an actively managed fund, it's unlikely to underperform. And because an ETF charges annual fees at an average of 0.23 percent of the funds invested against an average of 1.45 percent for actively managed mutual funds, the investor gets almost all the performance of the underlying stocks.

The difference between the ETF's fees and the mutual fund's fees (1.22 percent) might not seem like a lot of money. But remember, that's an annual charge, and over ten years, it could add up to more than 12 percent of the value of the funds.

It's a different way of looking at the market than Buffett. Where Bogle and Buffett would agree, though, is that an investment is a long-term game.

In fact, Buffett thinks an indexing approach works, though it's not the way he personally operates. He made a bet against hedge fund manager Ted Seides that an S&P (Standard and Poor's) index fund would outperform the hedge fund. He won $2.2 million on his bet and donated it to Girls Inc., a charity in Omaha, Nebraska.

Buffett also recommends a "90/10" portfolio for most investors. Ninety percent goes to low-cost S&P 500 index funds and the remainder to short-term bonds. In his view, that gives investors the right balance between the safety of bonds and the growth potential of stocks, but it only works if you don't chop and change.

One investor who is less well known for his investing prowess than for his other achievements is the economist John Maynard Keynes. He's a particularly good role model for ordinary, fallible humans because he made a couple of false starts before finding his feet.

Keynes wasn't immune to bear markets, and he started out as a speculator, using what he called "credit cycle" investments. Nowadays, we would call this momentum investing. He aimed to spot what the market was doing, then ride the wave before bowing out before investors changed their minds. He also started out trading on margin; on at least one occasion, he had to borrow money to keep his trading fund solvent.

He lost a great deal of his first fortune in the 1929 crash. But he reacted quickly, hoping his previous strategy would work out. Within a few years, he was back in profit and on his way to making a second fortune. He also changed his investment style, reducing debt and becoming a value investor focused on the long term. Keynes had a focused portfolio, looking for a concentrated number of great ideas and buying stocks that looked cheap compared to their ultimate earning power.

While Keynes came to dividend investment ("an activity of forecasting the yield over the life of the asset") from speculation ("the activity of forecasting the psychology of the market"), whether he was investing or speculating, he was a contrarian. He thought through his investments from first principles and did not accept conventional thinking.

As First Bursar of King's College Cambridge, he took the college funds out of agricultural lands and government stocks and put them into equity investing. King's College was one of Cambridge's less wealthy colleges when he started. By the time he'd finished, it was among the top three. But it's interesting that he seems to have made slightly different decisions for the college and for himself. This underlines the fact that investment is about the investor as much as it is about the investment. That's the same idea as Buffett investing directly in a concentrated bunch of companies but recommending a 90/10 portfolio for most individual investors.

Each of these investors has a slightly different way of approaching the market, though they draw on a common background. They all look at the business underneath the stock rather than at the stock price. Some look at earnings power, others at dividends or book value, but they are all looking to pick up a bargain, a stock that is worth more than the share price. In short, they are all value investors.

What is particularly interesting about writing this book in mid-2022 is that for several years before 2020, many investors had been saying that value investing no longer worked. Growth stocks were outperforming, with the FAANGS (Facebook, Amazon, Apple, Netflix, and Google) seeing returns significantly above the market. The Nasdaq 100 index, which is heavily weighted toward technology stocks, returned around 16 percent a year compared with just 8 percent from the more general S&P 500 for nearly two decades.

However, in late 2020, things began to change. Value stocks began to outperform. There may be several reasons. First, the valuations of value stocks had become extremely cheap. Secondly, the initial bounce from the early 2020 correction had been exhausted, so some investors were looking to de-risk their portfolios. Thirdly, with interest rates likely to rise, growth stocks looked riskier. (Growth stocks are longer duration assets, as valuations are based on future cash flows that may be five years out or more, so interest rates affect their valuation more than value stocks.) But the result is that value investors who had kept their faith saw their portfolios outperform, and they managed to do less poorly than the market when the S&P 500 started to move downward in 2022.

All of these investors also knew what they were good at and concentrated on doing more of the same. Geraldine Weiss hit her stride very quickly, while Keynes took nearly twenty years to learn by getting his fingers burned. They also had discipline, whether that came in the shape of a detailed quantitative screening process like the one Weiss used or a more qualitative approach to stocks as used by Lynch and Buffett.

However, both Lynch and Buffett may have made a mistake by staying out of all technology stocks. No doubt some of the dot coms were run on flimsy business models, but technology is an important part of our lives today. There's really no excuse for not understanding it. (Warren Buffett possibly would not be able to explain how airplane engines work or how planes actually fly, but he invests in airlines.)

In fact, Buffett has changed his mind on tech. The tech sector has become more stable, and the bad business models have been weeded out, but Buffett, because he's an intelligent guy and a smart investor, has recognized that things have changed. He set out to learn what he needed to invest in. He now holds Apple and Amazon shares. In fact, he is one of Apple's biggest shareholders.

That's something all the great investors have in common. They were willing to admit and learn from their mistakes. Read Lynch's books, and you'll get as many horror stories about the great investment that got away or the stock he lost a lot of money on as you will stories about successful investments. He always examines his losing decisions and explains why they went wrong. Sometimes, he had a good reason for investing, but sometimes, he hadn't noticed a weakness in the business. Or he loved the business but didn't buy in because he thought it was too expensive and missed the boat.

Hindsight, of course, is 20/20, and we all know investors who "could've been a contender" if only Bitcoin hadn't crashed. "Coulda, shoulda, woulda" is useless in the investment arena. But learning from your mistakes is not about comforting yourself. It's about confronting your mistake and examining how you could have avoided it. You might also consider whether that mistake shows you have a built-in bias of which you need to be aware.

For instance, if you have a losing run of investments, ask yourself why each individual investment went wrong, and try to find the common factors. It may be that you're looking for too high a return. There's some evidence that investors buying REITs that yield between 4 percent and 6 percent do better than those who search for high-yield REITs paying 8 percent or more. That's because the very high-yield stock has been priced by the market as a weak operator with poor prospects; the market might even expect that it will cut its dividends. If you invested in three of these companies in a row, you might have seen all of them doing badly.

You could go a little bit further and look to see if the companies have other factors in common, such as high indebtedness or lack of dividend cover. You might then be able to set up a screen to exclude companies that have these negative aspects. Or you might concentrate on the slightly lower-yield companies, where you are more likely to be buying quality.

By analyzing what you did wrong, how you might have spotted the problems, and how you can change your investment focus or process in the future, you are actively engaging with your past decisions and with your future.

5 ways to use hindsight to your advantage

1. Review the reasons why you made a poor investment (or didn't make a good investment). Did you ignore or miss any factors that might have led to an alternative decision? If so, how can you ensure those factors are included in your analysis next time you assess an investment?

2. Was there a point at which you could have exited the investment with a profit or at a smaller loss? For instance, if you held on to a stock after the first profit downgraded only to see two more downgrades in quick succession, then you had two opportunities to exit. Why didn't you?

3. Write an investment diary. Every time you make an investment decision, note down your reasoning. That way, you will be clear about why you chose that investment. Write down ideas that you decided, for whatever reason, not to pursue. Review your investment diary as part of your regular investment review process.

4. Have a regular review process! It needs to be somewhere between every month and every half year; every quarter works well, particularly if you do your review just after the main results season. Don't just look at stock prices. Look at results, valuations, and dividends. Stock prices are much less important than the business results.

5. Avoid hindsight bias. Investors have a tendency to think after a few winning investments that they have a golden touch. Looking back, if you bought Apple because you liked the name rather than because you liked the business, that was a bad decision, even if it worked out well for you. Always consider the reasons behind your performance rather than the performance itself.

By the way, it may be helpful to take a couple of great men as your negative models for investment. Isaac Newton, who lost a huge amount of money in the South Sea Bubble, is one. To paraphrase his commentary, knowing math and doing the right calculations is useless if the market is completely irrational. If, on the other hand, he'd recognized that the market was irrational, he might have saved his money.

The other great negative role model is French writer Marcel Proust. He was a great writer. He was a terrible investor. He did have a method, though. He bought shares with interesting and evocative names. It's a method that simply does not work.

Chapter 7: Mansa Musa: Lessons from the Man That Had It All

"Not sayin' I'm the richest man alive, but I'm in the game." -Wiz Khalifa

In 1312, Europe was a mess. The Holy Roman emperor had to be crowned in the Lateran, Rome's number two church, because the Vatican was occupied by the king of Naples. St. Peter's was, therefore, not available. Partisans of different local factions were fighting in the streets. The powerful and wealthy order of the Knights Templar was being disbanded by the pope, who was in cahoots with the king of France, who had his eyes on the knights' treasure. In England, King Edward II's favorite Piers Gaveston had just been hunted down and executed by the earl of Warwick, nearly leading to civil war. Europe was fragmented and unstable.

Meanwhile, in Africa, the Mali Empire was flourishing. When Musa ibn Abi-Bakr succeeded the throne, becoming Mansa Musa, in 1312, he was the ninth king in line from the empire's founder Sunjata (Sundiata) Keita, his great-uncle.

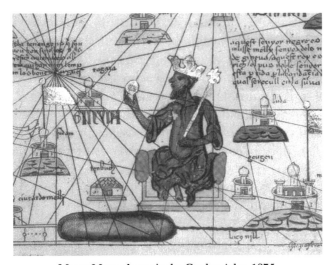
Mansa Musa, shown in the Catalan Atlas, 1375.
https://commons.wikimedia.org/wiki/File:Mansa_Musa.jpg

Mansa Musa was not only born into the extended royal family, but he apparently had been ruling the empire as regent for the previous mansa. The eighth mansa was more of an explorer than an emperor. He was fascinated by the question of what lay beyond the Atlantic and put together a fleet and set out, 180 years before Christopher Columbus had the same idea. He never came back.

He might have discovered America, though no Malian artifacts have ever been found there. He might have perished at sea. Or Mansa Musa might have had the ships scuttled as soon as they left the harbor. No one knows. But Musa went on to become the greatest of all Mali's emperors.

He was also widely reputed to be the world's richest man.

So, how did he do it? And are there lessons for us today in what he achieved?

* * *

One thing we know is that he had excellent PR. As a good Muslim, Mansa Musa decided to make the hajj, taking a huge caravan on his pilgrimage up through Egypt and onward to the holy city of Mecca. He is said to have taken sixty thousand other pilgrims with him, together with five hundred personal slaves. Some said the caravan was so long you could not see one end of it from the other.

This was impressive, but what was even more impressive was the astonishing amount of wealth he took with him, mostly in gold. Reports vary. He had a hundred camels laden with gold. Or perhaps it was a thousand camels, each carrying a hundred pounds of gold. Or five hundred slaves, each carrying rods of gold that weighed four and a half pounds. Or the slaves and then another three hundred camels with even more gold. One history claims he took 60,000, porters each carrying 6 pounds of gold, which would make 180 tons. (For comparison, Fort Knox has just over five thousand tons of gold, but Musa lived in the days before huge open cast mines and bulldozers, before Europe discovered the rich mineral reserves of the Americas, and in an empire only about the size of Alaska.)

As Marc de Villiers says in his book on Timbuktu, "Which of these [estimates of Mansa Musa's wealth], if any, is 'true' is of course unknown."

However much gold he took with him, it was enough to impress the merchants of Cairo. Mansa Musa is said to have spent and given away so much money that he wrecked the Egyptian economy. Historian Ibn Khaldun, writing about fifty years later, calls Mansa Musa "the richest man in the world." Though some of his information is inconsistent with what we know from other sources, this assertion is borne out by other sources.

Mansa Musa had inherited a great empire. These were West Africa's golden years. Caravans of gold, salt, and ivory crisscrossed the Sahara. Mali was fertile and wealthy and created a classical culture that is still celebrated today. (If you've ever listened to a kora player like Toumani Diabate or Sona Jobarteh, you're listening to music that has been preserved for generations by griots or praise singers. They still sing the Sunjata Keita, the story of the first mansa of Mali.)

But it wasn't enough for Mansa Musa. He set out on a campaign of conquest, which expanded the empire's boundaries to their farthest extent. The Empire of Mali included the modern countries of Guinea, Senegal, Guinea-Bissau, Ivory Coast, and the Gambia, together with parts of Mauritania, Burkina Faso, Niger, and Ghana. His empire had over four hundred cities and large towns. It was fully urbanized and had a sophisticated administration for each province.

Musa appears to have had a smart strategy for conquest. Although his original capital was Niani, located in the headwaters of the Niger River, this wasn't the commercial center of Africa at the time. So, he set out to control the entrepots through which trade was channeled: Gao and Timbuktu. Gao dominated the trade to the south and east, including a number of rich goldfields, while Timbuktu dealt with North Africa, including the important salt mines. He then encouraged Timbuktu to become an even more important nexus of trade, attracting Hausa merchants from the east and Egyptians from the north and developing strong links with both the Mamluk sultanate in Egypt and the Marinids in Morocco.

In fact, had he wanted to, he could have taken over the Gold Coast, where a lot of the major gold mines were located. He didn't. And he was right to do so, as leaving the area's autonomy intact kept gold production high. All he needed was to own the miners' routes to markets.

Mansa Musa's Mali was a highly cosmopolitan empire. We often think of Africa before Western colonialization as being dominated by single tribes, but Mali included a wide mixture of ethnicities: the Songhai in Gao, Bambara, Malinke, Soninke, Fulani, and others. It was an Islamic empire but sophisticated in nature. Arabic letters allowed scholars to write not just Arabic but also local languages.

An image of Mansa Musa.

HistoryNmoor, CC BY-SA 4.0 <https://creativecommons.org/licenses/by-sa/4.0>, via Wikimedia Commons: https://commons.wikimedia.org/wiki/File:Empire_mansa_musa.jpeg

Mansa Musa was also clear about the importance of education. He promoted Timbuktu as a seat of learning, attracting scholars from the rest of the Islamic world. Jurists, astronomers, and mathematicians headed to Timbuktu, which became a major university center and held huge libraries of manuscripts, many of which have been passed down through the main families of the city. He is even said to have attracted poets and architects from the Andalusian court of Spain.

His building program included a palace for himself, naturally, but he also erected the Djinguereber Mosque in Timbuktu and the Sankoré Madrasah (an Islamic school).

How would Mansa Musa's strategies work today? Probably quite well, though he would have to rely on hostile takeovers or venture capital rather than on warriors carving out his empire.

His first strategy, controlling natural resources and trade by controlling the caravan routes, might have led him to focus on investing in oil pipelines, refineries, ports, or airports if he was alive today. Alternatively, he might focus on the internet and media, aiming to own content delivery channels. What he wouldn't be doing is digging for gold or writing film scripts. The "gatekeeper" strategy can work extremely well. Though, in a faster changing world, it can be riskier (think of the AT&T and Time Warner merger, which was a disaster for shareholders).

Or maybe, Mansa Musa would be running a multinational bank, channeling investment funds, or providing trade services, such as letters of credit, trade insurance, and escrow. He'd be in the First Bank of Nigeria or Senegal's Bank of Africa Group, or he'd be running a mobile payment system like M-Pesa. He would be taking a tiny slice of every transaction, just as he took a tiny tax from each caravan passing through his empire.

Mansa Musa also understood the importance of knowledge. By sourcing talent from the cultural centers of Europe and the Near East, he was ensuring that his empire could benefit from the best and newest technology. The fact that many of his ambitious buildings are still standing today reflects the engineering prowess of his time, although they have, of course, been restored many times.

One factor that might reduce Mansa Musa's wealth nowadays, though, is the separation of public and private goods and the separation between shareholders' wealth and that of company management. Mansa Musa, as king, inherited the immense wealth of the Mali Empire; there was no distinction made between his personal inheritance and the state treasury. He would almost certainly have considerably more limited means today, and he'd also have to deliver a more comprehensive set of accounts.

In fact, he might even have to pay taxes.

Chapter 8: Influential Empires and Emperors

"All empire is no more than power in trust." - John Dryden

Money has a dual nature; it's a medium of exchange, but it's also a store of wealth. You might use a couple of dollar bills or a mobile payment to grab your morning Starbucks, but you might go without your caffeine for a while and put the savings into a brokerage account.

Cryptocurrencies are the same. You could have used a few bitcoins to buy yourself a beer back in 2010, or you could have held on to them.

Both of these jobs have also been done by other objects. In many pastoral communities, cattle have been used as a source of wealth, as well as a means of exchange. In early Celtic societies, most crimes incurred fines that were paid in cattle (in fact, the unit of exchange was a Sét, that is, half the value of a milk cow).

The Aztec economy had a form of money (cocoa beans), though these were used as spare change, as the Aztecs depended predominantly on the barter system. But a great deal of the economy's wealth ended up in the temples. For instance, Aztec merchants would buy sacrificial victims, such as slaves or prisoners of war, and treat them as honored guests, feeding them well. They would then have them sacrificed and serve the flesh at a feast; the owner of the victim was strictly forbidden from partaking.

Another example of a barter system was 1980s Italy. The smallest coins were worth more if they had a hole in the middle and were more used as washers or gaskets than they were as coins. So, if you went to the supermarket, small change would be provided in the form of tiny wrapped sweets. You might buy a bottle of wine, some ham, bread, and a tin of tuna, hand over a note, and get three strawberry flavor gums as change. (If you were unlucky, you got lime.)

Ancient Egypt was one of the first command economies, where prices and investments are dictated by a central governing body. It wasn't a monetary economy until late in its history, but it developed an accounting system and an obsession with counting and tallying. For instance, Egyptian tombs and temples have huge offering tables showing how much particular donors gave to the gods, such as how many loaves of bread or sacrificial oxen.

Offering table of Tjaenhesret.
Metropolitan Museum of Art, CC0, via Wikimedia Commons:
https://commons.wikimedia.org/wiki/File:Offering_Table_of_Tjaenhesret,_priest_of_Thot
h,_son_of_Iaa_MET_DP244258.jpg

Grain appears to have been stored in temple granaries or state warehouses. Beer jars and loaf sizes were standardized so that bread and beer could be used to pay for hours of work or for other goods.

Egypt became extremely wealthy, but that wealth appears to have been directed mainly toward the cult of the dead. While temples received rich gifts from the pharaohs, they were only a sideshow to the immense pyramids. Later on, kings like Tutankhamun were buried with immense amounts of gold and jewels, as well as furniture and household equipment.

So, you might ask what wealth is. Having a tomb full of gold? Owning four prisoners of war? Medieval African kings might have said it was a treasury full of salt. And under Nicolae Ceausescu, many Romanians would have stored their worldly wealth in the form of packets of Western cigarettes.

* * *

However, there's another aspect to money. As well as being used for exchange or to store wealth, it can be used to *create* wealth through investment. That's something Egypt didn't do. It's also something that early modern France was not good at.

There's some evidence that in the 17th century, France was ahead of England in engineering. The great Machine of Marly drew water up from the Seine to the plateau at Versailles to feed the fountains of the royal palace. Louis XIV even had a railway, a century before rails were thought of in England; it was called La Roulette and seems to have been half railway, half roller-coaster.

The trouble was these engines were used purely for frivolous display. They weren't used for manufacturing or transport but just for fun. It's as if we had invented computers and only used them to play Donkey Kong.

(Today, though, France does benefit from the luxury trades that were established by Louis's first minister, Jean-Baptiste Colbert. He set up the Gobelins tapestry factory and a royal glassmaking workshop. Previously, France had to import all its mirror glass from Venice. This set a precedent that was followed later by Louis XV, who set up the Sèvres porcelain factory. France is still a global leader in the luxury trade, with brands such as Hermès, Louis Vuitton, Chanel, Cartier, and Dior.)

On the other hand, when steam engines and railways were invented in Britain, they were immediately applied to manufacturing and mining. The Industrial Revolution could have happened in

France, but it didn't, simply because the French nobility had no interest in productivity.

* * *

The Roman Empire developed out of an agricultural economy based on grain and wine production. Rome was originally one among many city-states in Italy, founded by different peoples, including Greek colonizers and indigenous Etruscans and Latins. What differentiated Rome from the others was its drive for military conquest. Gradually, it took over most of the other cities in central Italy, and by the time the Roman Republic gave way to the Roman Empire, it had extended around the Mediterranean and up as far as Gaul, Germany, and Britain.

This gave Rome access to natural resources like gold and silver (Gaul, Spain, Macedonia), tin (Asia Minor, Britain), and iron (Gaul), as well as foreign luxury goods and foodstuffs. The Romans built major infrastructure that served military, administrative, and commercial purposes all at the same time, such as the huge Roman roads and massive ports like Ostia (at the mouth of the Tiber, downstream from the city of Rome).

Rome developed some major technologies that assisted its growth. For instance, hydraulic mining allowed the Romans to extract minerals more efficiently, using ground-sluicing and hushing or booming (planned flooding) instead of digging to clear large amounts of earth. Building at scale was enabled by the discovery of concrete, as well as the manufacture of brick and tile.

Surveying technology was a particular strength of the Romans, who probably inherited many techniques from the earlier Etruscan civilization. This enabled them to create large-scale waterworks to feed their cities, as well as a network of roads that, in many cases, still dictate the course of today's major highways.

While much of the Roman economy remains a mystery, we do know there was a working credit system. It is commonly believed that anyone doing any kind of business in the Roman Empire needed access to credit. The elite senatorial families used their inherited wealth to lend funds to business ventures and often acted as full-scale banks. We also know from tombstones and other evidence that tradesmen often used credit to build up major businesses and to enter commercial relations with other parts of the empire.

This relatively advanced mixed economy may be one reason why Rome was able to take over such a large empire.

Italian Renaissance

Christianity, like Islam, did not like banks. The principle of giving or taking interest was described as "usury" and was considered sinful, which is one reason Jews were often the main lenders in early medieval economies.

However, by the 14th century, northern Italy was beginning to develop an operational banking system. The small city-states and republics of this area had flourishing commerce, both within Italy and with northern states, since they were on the route to Rome, the center of the Catholic Church. Family banks began to serve the needs of trade.

They worked in the marketplace rather than from fortresses (as, for instance, the Templars had). The very word "bank" comes from *banco*, or bench. They would trade bills of exchange to traveling merchants, charging around 10 percent of the total as a commission. This avoided the merchants having to transport coinage in gold or silver, which meant they could travel faster (cutting a three-week trip from France to Rome down to eight days) and be more secure. Besides, bills of exchange could be issued in any currency.

The Peruzzi and Bardi families of Florence, for instance, financed King Edward I and King Edward II of England in their wars against Wales and Scotland. The Church in London banked its money with them, and they sent bills of exchange to Rome while keeping the deposits in London so that they could trade in wool, England's biggest export.

During this period, the system of double-entry bookkeeping that's still used today was invented, as was the check. Fibonacci introduced Arabic numerals to Pisa in 1202, including the useful zero, and further progress in mathematics was driven by merchants' needs.

This led to an emphasis on education, particularly in Florence. It's easy to look at the Florentine townscape today and think it's quaint, beautiful, and elegant; in fact, buildings, such as the cathedral with its huge dome, relied on intricate engineering calculations and craft traditions. Secular education to train mathematicians, politicians, and administrators took over medieval education, which was mainly intended to create priests. Books of science were translated from Greek and sometimes from Arabic. Papermakers, scribes, and (later) printers found a ready market for their wares.

A great deal of money was spent on architecture and public spaces, including town halls, market arcades, bridges, hospitals, churches, and cloisters. Leon Battista Alberti, one of the leading architects of the period, stated that architecture was designed to create a harmonious environment that would allow people to live in a civilized and fruitful way—very much like Le Corbusier's 20th-century assertion that a house is a *machine-à-habiter*, a machine for living in.

Florentine politics was very fluid for a long time. It was linked to the ongoing conflicts between the Holy Roman emperor (who, despite being called "Roman," had his base in Germany) and the pope, with Florentine families taking one side or the other. At times, half the leading families would be in exile. Then, in 1397, Giovanni de' Medici, who had been working for another bank in Rome, set up his own bank in Florence. His son, Cosimo, became the effective ruler of Florence.

But since Florence was a republic, Cosimo never claimed any public office. He built a palace that, while luxurious, looked very similar to the other noble families' palaces. He sponsored scholars, painters, and sculptors and founded the first public library in the city. His main personal luxury was his extensive book collection. He seems to have been opposed to bling; it sent the wrong political message for a man who wanted to be seen as the best of citizens.

Cosimo de' Medici.
https://commons.wikimedia.org/wiki/File:Cosimo_di_Medici_(Bronzino).jpg

Florence never developed into an empire; it remained a trading city. This partly may have been because the bank was run by lesser men after Cosimo, such as Piero "the Gouty" and Lorenzo the Magnificent, both of whom spent more than they made. Later, the Medici became dukes of Florence—albeit backed by a Medici pope—but they had only a fragment of the power of their ancestor Cosimo.

This is the story of many family businesses. The first generation or two are entrepreneurs, creating a new business, innovating, and growing it fast. Then come the capable administrators, who may still be able to run the business but probably spend more time on PR than on doing the accounts. And finally, the business ends up in the hands of a spoiled child whose expensive education hasn't really prepared him to run the business. Only in the case of Florence, the family business and the republic were so interwoven that it's difficult to tell where one ends and the other begins.

The British Empire

For most of the Middle Ages, England and Scotland were small kingdoms off the edge of Europe. They were of relatively little relevance and rather outrageous in nature (the French believed that Englishmen had tails for a long time). Things began to change in the 16th century.

Edward VI, the son of the more famous Henry VIII, isn't known for much. He died at the age of fifteen, and most of his policies were reversed by his successor, Mary Tudor. However, as a Protestant monarch, Edward founded a number of grammar schools, taking education out of the hands of the church and vastly expanding literacy. Humanistic education included not just grammar and Latin but also some elements of natural sciences, history, and geography. This created a well-educated class of townsmen and gentry.

Under Elizabeth I, Mary's successor, education continued to be a priority. This coincided with the Age of Exploration. English sailors ventured to South and North America and attempted to find the Northwest Passage, while Tom Coryate walked all the way to India (and wrote about it). England was becoming a major naval power and a big commercial player as well, trading with the Americas and the East. However, this was still preparation for the country's future; the major powers in Europe remained France and Spain.

England had one big advantage during the 17th century; it was beginning to put its capital to use. The city of London became an immense engine of commerce; its only rival was Amsterdam. The rest of Europe was falling way behind the financial innovations of these two centers. For instance, the joint stock company replaced single-voyage financing, and there was also a strong banking system.

However, Napoleon's overthrow at Waterloo put Britain (which included Scotland, Ireland, England, and Wales at this point) at the forefront in military and diplomatic terms. Britain was now the leading power in Europe. It was increasing its territory in India and began to colonize Africa over the next century. Its previous investments in maritime power gave it a merchant navy to carry trade and the military means to defend its merchant ships.

Britain turned its colonies into huge commodity producers. It then imported those commodities, added value to them—for instance, making textiles from Indian cotton in Manchester—and then re-exported them to the colonies. Tariffs discouraged colonial businesses from competing in the finished products trade. By the mid-19th century, Britain had 20 percent of the world's income and 40 percent of global exports.

France had also acquired colonies in the Pacific and in India, though it eventually lost its Indian territories. However, London had one great advantage that Paris couldn't match. It was a major financial center. When the French government needed finances, it issued bonds in London. By becoming the financial center of Europe, London ensured Britain's dominance. The pound sterling became a reserve currency, and London remained the center of the financial world even after the US started to gain dominance in military and commercial life.

The sterling area (countries that used sterling as currency or fixed their currencies to sterling) lasted longer than the British Empire. However, decolonization, together with multiple devaluations, stripped the pound of its value. After the Second World War, the dollar succeeded sterling's position as the world's top currency.

It's interesting to see how certain advantages in education and finance played out over two or three centuries to create the British Empire. It's also interesting to see that Britain remained a key financial player after the demise of the empire; many American and European stocks are listed on the London Stock Exchange even today. However, Britain's decision to leave the European Union has reduced it to a much less influential player on the world scene. Could the days of Hope and Glory be over?

One Maharaja's Story

A single decision can have long-term effects. In Travancore, a kingdom in southern India, the maharaja made an unusual decision to spend a good part of his budget on building schools instead of buying elephants. Meanwhile, the Rajput maharajas of the north were spending their money on luxuries. They built new palaces, hired huge retinues of servants, and bought expensive jewelry and silks.

Kerala, which took over most of Travancore's territory, remains the Indian state with the highest literacy rate. Almost 94 percent of Keralans can read and write; Rajasthan is way behind, with a literacy rate of only 67 percent. Kerala remains one of the top ten states by GDP per capita and has a growing IT industry; Rajasthan ranks much lower, with its GDP per capita only about half the level of Kerala's in 2019/20, according to the Reserve Bank of India. Many Keralans now spend the first part of their careers working in the Gulf States, earning high, tax-free salaries and sending regular remittances to their families. Others get green cards and work in the US. FedEx CEO Raj Subramaniam was born and brought up in Kerala, as was Thomas Kurian, who is the current CEO of Google Cloud as of mid-2022.

* * *

We've seen how different countries utilized their wealth. Spending on education and innovation is paramount. The two need to be put together. For example, ancient Egypt appears to have had a high literacy rate but very limited innovations.

It's slightly old-fashioned history, but the Reformation appears to have made a change in European history. Protestant emphases on education (for reading the Bible) and self-determination (individualism) helped create an entrepreneurial culture in both the Netherlands and Britain. When Louis XIV got rid of the Huguenot Protestants by revoking the Edict of Nantes (the law of religious tolerance), he exiled some of the country's best weavers, merchants, and businessmen.

So, how can you apply these principles to your life? One way is to invest in your own education and skills. That might mean qualifying as a physician, or it might mean learning craft skills or technology applications that you could use in a side hustle. It may mean putting yourself forward at work for extra training even though time is tight. In fact, though it was not included as a way of safeguarding assets in times of war, it's worth noting that many medics, lawyers, scientists, artists, and other professionals fleeing war-torn countries were able to regain their former lifestyle, despite having to leave most of their hard-earned assets and cash behind.

The other thing you should do is to put your capital at the service of innovation. That means investing in innovative businesses, whether they're tech businesses, services, or manufacturing companies that are using new approaches to cut costs or improve quality. Green energy, recycling, and electric vehicles are innovations that will help reduce global warming. Self-driving cars, artificial intelligence, and cloud computing are all likely to change the way we live. Buy shares in good businesses, and if you have enough capital and expertise, become an "angel" or invest in venture funds.

And you might consider investing in a couple of Kickstarter projects too.

Chapter 9: The Rush for Gold: Is Money Losing Its Identity?

"How gold may be best extracted. By supplying, at exorbitant prices, the wants of those who gather it." - The Sydney Morning Herald

If there's one thing that has driven mankind from the earliest days, it's the dream of gold. From the story of Jason and the Golden Fleece to tales of El Dorado and the goose that laid the golden egg, gold has beckoned explorers, investors, miners, veterans, blacksmiths, and farm boys—and they've followed its gleam. Some have become rich, but most have been disappointed.

The California Gold Rush began in 1848 when John Sutter decided to put up a sawmill at his settlement in Coloma. The man digging the trench for the mill saw something gleaming in the mud. It was gold! Within days, everyone knew what had happened, and the first miners were already staking their claims.

It was easy. All you needed was a pick, a shovel, a pan (Native Americans used baskets instead), and running water. You shoveled dirt into the pan and swished it around in the water. The dirt would be carried off, and the heavier gold would be left in the bottom of the pan. You didn't need much money, you didn't need a fancy education, and you didn't need to know the right people. You just needed to get there.

Miners in the California Gold Rush, 1850.
https://commons.wikimedia.org/wiki/File:1850_Woman_and_Men_in_California_Gold_Rush.jpg

People headed to California from the east, from Mexico, and even from France, Australia, and China. The number of miners and claims exploded. At Dry Diggings, there were fifty log cabins in 1848; within a year, there were more than two thousand camps and huts.

Some men became rich, and some even became rich by accident. Explorer James C. Fremont thought he had settled down to enjoy his life on a ranch when gold was found on his Mariposa ranch. He became the first senator for the new state of California and served as governor for Arizona but ended up losing much of his wealth investing in railways.

Mining was hard. The pace of work was frenetic. Most miners wouldn't even take the time to build a cabin because they could spend that time working on their claim. And there was a 25 percent mortality rate in the camps, with cholera being one of the biggest killers. Then, of course, there was luck. In Bear Valley, a team of Mexicans struck huge gold reserves. Their success attracted over four hundred miners, but all the claims around the central one failed. By the end of the month, the twelve Mexicans were on their own again.

There was another way to do well, and that was to provide what miners needed. This became known as the "picks and shovels" strategy, but people didn't need just picks and shovels. Horses, mules, alcohol, beans, blankets, and women were all in high demand and sold at crazily high prices. According to one report, a spade that would sell for a dollar was sold at $10 in the gold regions and could even fetch $50 if stocks ran low.

Samuel McNeil started off as a miner but found that life was simply too hard. He ended up establishing a shop, the Sycamore Tree Establishment. He cleared $1,500 in profit, then sold the joint for $400 and went home to Ohio. Al Swearengen set up a canvas tent saloon in Deadwood before establishing the much larger Gem Theater; he could make as much as $10,000 a night. Running a restaurant, a boardinghouse, or a saloon could be a passport to a fortune. M. L. Winn served up to five thousand customers a day in his two San Francisco diners.

You didn't need to be in California to make money. New York merchants sold "essentials" to those heading for the goldfields, including life jackets, pots, frying pans, water filters, rifles, handguns, hatchets, powder pouches, shot, and lead. Towns on the Missouri River, such as Independence and St. Joseph, where emigrants crossed, charged double or triple St. Louis's price for basic goods. Printers sold guidebooks to California.

Samuel Brannan diversified. He started with a Sacramento store, then built hotels, warehouses, and the first wharf in San Francisco. Brannan also developed Napa Valley and Calistoga Springs as tourist centers. He started overland mail to the east and even brought the first steam locomotive to California (by sea). He was a creator of infrastructure and became one of the richest and most influential men in California. (Later, he also became a brewer, but drinking his own production proved to be his downfall.)

As for John Augustus Sutter, on whose land that first gold was found, he missed the boat. He kept trying to make agriculture and the sawmill work and to attract trade to his trading post at Fort Sutter, Coloma, but the cheap labor he needed to make his businesses operate had poor tools and had set off to the goldfields. Worse, Sacramento took over the trading post business simply because it was on the river. Worse still, he couldn't prove his title to the land because he'd set up the business under Mexican rule before California had become part of the United States. Congress eventually voted to give him compensation, but he died before receiving it.

The California Gold Rush was all over by 1855; it lasted barely more than a decade.

* * *

"Picks and shovels" (and "women and whiskey") were a surer way than gold mining to make money in California. But they had their risks too.

For instance, if you set up a bar and the lode ran out, the miners would look for better opportunities. You would have a bar in a ghost town, which is not a profitable venture. Being nimble and moving on to the next thing was important. This applied to the gold diggers as well; for instance, George Hearst moved on from gold mining in California to Nevada, where he made an even bigger fortune.

Technologies changed. At first, miners used sheath knives to pry out nuggets of gold. Then, panning came along, but that was quickly replaced by the California cradle or rocker box, then by the Long Tom, and then by full-scale damming and dredging of watercourses (hydraulic mining). Along with the development of technologies, the mining business moved the stage at which one man could run his own claim. You needed two or three men to use a Long Tom, while full-scale damming needed a large team of diggers and more money because it took months until the site was ready to start mining. But the cost of processing a cubic yard of dirt by panning was $20; with hydraulic mining, it was just twenty cents. Eventually, the big mining companies took over. It wasn't picks and shovels that made money anymore; it was conveyors and crushers.

The infrastructure supporting the Gold Rush changed too. Steamship companies made a fortune bringing the intrepid adventurers to the goldfields, but as soon as the Union Pacific and Continental Pacific railroads got going in the 1870s, the steamships had lost their market. (Wells Fargo, though, retained its dominance, moving from express gold and mail shipments to full-scale banking.)

But one thing hadn't changed. The little town of Yerba Buena had grown into San Francisco, and San Francisco managed to grow from a transit camp into a full-scale city. It was the big winner of the Gold Rush.

* * *

The Gold Rush happened all over again in the 1990s. This time, the real estate being carved up wasn't mining claims but access to the internet.

It started in 1991 when Tim Berners-Lee created a decentralized, hyperlinked system of documents. That may not sound like much, but hyperlinking meant that knowledge could be more easily found, and decentralization meant more people could feed their expertise and knowledge into the system. By 1993, there were fourteen million people online. By 1999, that had grown to 281 million, and it tripled again by 2002. As of 2022, over 4.5 billion people have access to the internet.

It was a gold rush. And like the California Gold Rush, a lot depended on luck. A few claims paid out, but many more never produced a single nugget of gold.

Narratives of the "new era" made the traditional irrelevant, such as, for instance, the idea that a company should make a profit. Money was being invested everywhere without any clear strategy. There were some major stinkers among the deals. Webvan saw its valuation collapse from $31 billion to zero, and the AOL/Time Warner merger led to a $9 billion loss. (The CEO later called it the biggest mistake in corporate history.)

Picks and shovels did make money. For instance, Adobe, which created PostScript printer software, the PDF file format, and Photoshop, was able to purchase its main rival, Macromedia, in 2005. However, Adobe didn't rely only on the internet; it sold to the print sector too. Intel, Cisco, and other hardware companies also benefited from a solid corporate customer base and supplied hardware to "traditional" tech and experienced extra growth from the internet boom.

There were other areas that slipped under the radar but made money for smart investors, such as data centers, payment transfer systems, and cybersecurity.

But a lot of companies folded. Over half the dot-coms had folded or been bought by 2004. And even some of today's winners have lost their *initial* investors money. Priceline, which is now Booking Holdings, was initially valued at $23 billion and is now worth $74 billion. You might think that's a great result, but that took over twenty-two years. In the meantime, you could have picked up the shares for next to nothing from 2002 all the way to 2008—a period during which many early shareholders sold out for a loss of 90 percent or more.

Nonetheless, if you had invested in picks and shovels, you would have avoided some of the more egregious business models. You would not have bought online groceries, and you would not have bought Pets.com, eToys, Geocities, or theGlobe.com.

You wouldn't have bought Facebook or Amazon either. Unless you are certain they are going to outlast their competition (remember Myspace?), you are better off buying the picks and shovels. They might not make you rich fast, but you are at much less risk.

* * *

Now let's fast forward to cryptocurrencies, seen by some as the new Gold Rush. Bitcoin (BTC), the first cryptocurrency to gain traction, was launched in 2009 as a digital currency that does not rely on a central authority (like the Fed or the Bank of England) to maintain it. It uses a mix of technologies, including peer-to-peer networks, strong encryption, and blockchain. Blockchain is a bit difficult to explain, but if you think of an accounting ledger where both sides of every transaction are visible to whoever is authorized to see them, that's a pretty good way of visualizing it.

Bitcoin's price rose dramatically from 2009 onward. One early transaction was the use of 10,000 BTC to buy two Papa John's pizzas. Those were expensive pizzas; that amount of Bitcoin would be worth over $24,000 today.

However, Bitcoin was kind of like the Wild West, as the law wasn't always clear and wasn't always observed. Some countries, such as France, decided to regulate cryptocurrency exchanges; others, like Thailand and China, outlawed them. Buyers of crypto were at risk from bandits. The Mt. Gox exchange was hacked, first to send out fake bitcoins and later to steal 50,000 BTC. In 2014, it went bankrupt. Many of its users lost all their bitcoins.

Then, in 2018, the SEC decided all exchanges must be registered. Stripe stopped supporting Bitcoin transactions, and Google, Facebook, and Twitter all banned advertising for cryptocurrencies. Bitcoin's price collapsed from $18,000 to below $4,000. It's since recovered but remains very volatile.

Of course, Bitcoin isn't the only cryptocurrency. Ethereum, Tether, Cardano, Polkadot, and Dogecoin are some of the major names. (Dogecoin was originally a joke!) Some, like Bitcoin, have a hard cap on issuance; that is, once the currency reaches a certain issued amount, it cannot issue any more. Others, like Ethereum, are uncapped. Some are freely priced, while others, like Tether, are stablecoins. Tether is pegged to the dollar.

While Bitcoin was originally developed to be a means of exchange, right now, most cryptocurrencies are simply instruments of speculation. Their volatility makes them inefficient as a store of value compared with, say, holding AAA/AA-rated government bonds. That volatility, combined with high transaction costs, makes cryptocurrencies a poor means of exchange. Would you be happy to work not knowing what your salary will be at the end of the month? Or to sell a shirt not knowing what the exact price will be? Cryptocurrencies often go up or down 5 percent in a single day, so the difference could be substantial.

These reasons make it likely that cryptocurrencies aren't going to replace fiat money (government-backed currencies) any time soon. If you wanted to take a "picks and shovels" approach to crypto, you would have bought exchanges rather than currencies. But as the collapse of Mt. Gox and other exchanges shows, that wouldn't necessarily have avoided risk. Coinbase (COIN) is quoted on Nasdaq and accounts for over 10 percent of all crypto assets. It's regulated and has a $20.7 billion market capitalization, but it made a huge loss in the second quarter of 2022 when trading volumes dropped.

You could have bought Bitcoin mining company Riot Blockchain (RIOT), but again, its value is linked to that of Bitcoin. Silvergate Capital (SI), a provider of financial infrastructure solutions and services to participants in the digital currency industry, is a little less linked to cryptocurrency's price movements in the short term.

But why not look instead at the electronic enablers of ordinary fiat money? For instance, PayPal (PYPL) enables US users to buy and sell with four different cryptocurrencies, but it has also taken massive market shares away from traditional banks in money transfers between individuals. In Africa, M-Pesa has become a huge money transfer provider. It has gained huge market shares because banks are only represented in urban centers, but M-Pesa can be used in the villages and for tiny transactions since it uses mobile phone networks. Its co-owner Safaricom (SCOM) is quoted on the Nairobi Stock Exchange; its other owner, Vodaphone, is quoted in London and has stocks traded on Nasdaq, though M-Pesa is a much smaller part of its business.

The other interesting area to look at is blockchain. Cryptocurrencies are its most well-known implementation, but it has a lot of other uses. For instance, it could revolutionize the real estate transaction process by creating an open ledger accessible to realtors, attorneys, lenders, and their clients. That would cut out a huge amount of friction, such as telephone shunting, misaddressed emails, and lost files. According to one account, 90 percent of all major banks are now looking at using blockchain solutions.

Seattle's TaxBit is intriguing; it brings tax expertise and blockchain together to ensure cryptocurrencies and other digital assets can easily be integrated into corporate accounts and tax filings. NY-based Axoni uses blockchain as a collaborative technology for multi-party workflows, while Californian Spring Labs uses blockchain to enable faster, more secure information transfers between businesses.

If exchanges like Coinbase can start to leverage their blockchain expertise in other areas, they might transition to a very interesting model. But right now, they are special-purpose shovels, which can only be used for shoveling one very specific kind of dirt.

Cryptocurrency proponents tell us that crypto is going to change the world and that good old-fashioned money is on its way out. Crypto could be the new Gold Rush, and it might find real gold. On the other hand, it could be the new Tulipmania or South Sea Bubble. Where would you put *your* money?

Chapter 10: A New Age, An Old-World Order

"The experience of each new age requires a new confession." -Ralph Waldo Emerson

We can improve our technology. We can improve the liquidity of markets. We can improve regulation. But the one thing we can't change is us.

Human beings are still making the same old mistakes. People still jump on bandwagons the way they have since the tulip boom and the South Sea Bubble. People are still greedy, and greed still seems to stop brain cells from working properly. In the past twenty years or so, assets that have boomed and crashed include jatropha plantations for biofuel, Bulgarian ski chalets, e-vehicles, dot coms, buy-to-let homes in the UK, and now NFTs, cryptocurrencies, and even "digital land."

The whole history of GameStop has been presented very much as a "new world, new way of doing things." GameStop is a video game retailer that is attempting to pivot from bricks and mortar to online gaming using blockchain technology. However, in April 2022, the company had lost $400 million. A number of funds had shorted the stock, believing it was way overvalued. The short interest had gotten to 140 percent of the company's total capitalization—that is, nearly one and a half times more stock had been sold short than actually existed.

Users of the subreddit r/wallstreetbets, mainly young individual investors, decided it was time for a short squeeze—that is, sending the price up so that the funds that had shorted would be forced to buy stock to cover their positions. The price shot up from below $20 a share to over $300 a share within a couple of weeks. Then, suddenly, it fell back to $200 and then $50. Speculators who had bought in at the top went bust.

Because the squeeze was the work of younger traders, linked by a subreddit, using no-cost brokers like Robinhood, this was claimed to be something incredibly new and different. But it wasn't. It relied on the same tactics and the same market dynamics as Jay Gould's and John Fisk's attempt to "corner" the gold market—and that was back in *1869*.

Why don't people learn from history?

It is partly because they don't read enough history. Everybody has heard of the 1929 Wall Street Crash, but how many people have read JK Galbraith's *The Great Crash, 1929*? How many people have read different accounts of the Great Depression, looking at what actually happened to the US economy? How many of today's traders know what happened on Black Monday?

Reading economic history is particularly helpful because you can see those big patterns but also the smaller ones, and it gets your mind thinking about what actually made things work out in a particular order. It doesn't need to be stock market history; we've seen how Mansa Musa and the growth of the Roman Empire have lessons for us today. Read about colonialism, read about the medieval Hansa (a kind of forerunner of the EU, with member cities in several different European countries), or read about ancient Egypt or the Mughal invasion of India. If you treat it as the subject matter for thinking about economic and cultural processes rather than just picturesque backgrounds for Hollywood movies, you'll find there's a lot you can learn.

Interesting little bits of history are everywhere. In Amiens, a small plaque tells how in the Middle Ages, the city struck a free trade deal with the English city of Norwich. Norwich had wool, cloth, and dyers; Amiens had woad, a plant used to create blue dye. France and England are usually shown in history books as enemies, but that's not the full story. The two economies were linked in a number of interesting ways, including the wine trade in which English poet Geoffrey Chaucer was employed (but that's another story).

But another reason that people don't learn from history is that they think it will be different this time. That's often an emotional bias rather than an intellectual one.

For instance, people get FOMO—fear of missing out. I know a lot of people who didn't think they would enjoy *Game of Thrones*, and they didn't, but they kept watching because they thought any time, "real soon now," they would understand why their friends were raving about it. People rush to a new restaurant because they don't want to be the only ones who haven't tried it. They make bucket lists of places to see before they die.

They get carried away by emotions. One such emotion is greed. Some people sat out on GameStop initially. Then, they saw the price going up. Immediately, they thought about how much money they would have made *if only* they had invested right away. Some bought, while others waited. Some investors only gave in to that emotion just before GameStop shares hit $300 a share—they were the ones who lost really big money.

Fear is another big emotion that stops us from learning from our investment mistakes (and from other people's). It stops some people from ever investing. They say, "The stock market is really risky" or "I could lose all my money." What they should be doing, of course, is learning about risk and how to quantify it and learning about diversification and how to build a portfolio that includes cash, bonds, and stocks. But they don't. They just don't dare to put their toe in the water because they think the water will be too cold.

Other people are not like these worrywarts. They buy shares, some of them on the basis of tips or momentum, and some of them on the basis of their own research. They hold the shares, and they are happy. Most of them have a few losses in their investments. A few people get scared. Most of them think that a loss here or there is inevitable but that if the portfolio as a whole is doing well, that's what counts.

Then, the market takes a dip. And that's when the fear starts. Even the most sanguine investor will have a few bad nights of sleep. Nervous ones envision bankruptcy, their house auctioned off on the courtyard steps, having to tell their kids they can't have a college education. Some investors will sell out their weaker stocks fast, which is usually the smart thing to do in a real crash. Others will dither, hoping the price will go back up. Then, if it falls further, they'll sell, having lost more than they needed to.

Most of the fearful ones will remain fearful. Stocks will bottom out and be cheaply valued, but Mr. Scared and Ms. Worrywart won't buy any—they've been burned already. They will probably wait until the stocks hit another high to buy back in, right before the next crash.

An absolutely classic, completely irrational way of thinking is to attach every decision to the price at which you bought a share. The market does not care what you paid for your shares. What you paid does not represent value. But many investors remember this as the single most important fact about their investment.

They then display another irrational tendency, which is loss aversion. Most people find losing $20 makes them twice as upset as winning $20 makes them happy, so they aim to minimize losses rather than maximize gains. Sometimes, this makes people invest in "safe" assets like real estate, though, as you've seen, real estate can be every bit as risky as equities.

Loss aversion may, in some part, have led to the disaster of the Nifty Fifty. People were told that the companies they were buying shares in were great companies. And they believed that it was an investment without risk.

And then there's groupthink. One analyst who correctly predicted the subprime crisis was told by the bank, "Why should we believe you when the market's saying different?" That's a particularly egregious example. But very often, people do not do proper due diligence because they assume that someone else has done it. For instance, many of the people who invested in Bernie Madoff's fraudulent scheme did so because they were told that other people they knew had already done so or that their bank had done so.

Groupthink can lead to making a poor investment. It can also lead to feeling personally committed to that investment. The r/wallstreetbets crowd started believing in themselves as a kind of version of Robin Hood, as they stole from Wall Street to give to the poor (or rather, themselves). Once you let that kind of thinking into your head, rational arguments go out the window.

* * *

Another reason people don't learn from history is that it's different every time. A lot of people talk about "the Great Reset" or "the new world order." But it takes a long, long time for a new world order to happen. History rarely changes overnight.

For instance, when did the British Empire come to an end? Britain started losing its industrial and productive leadership to the US during the 19ᵗʰ century. If it hadn't been for the Civil War, the US might have gained leadership a good deal earlier. An amusing book entitled *1066 and All That*, published in 1930, looks at British history as a succession of "103 Good Things, 5 Bad Kings and 2 Genuine Dates." It ended with the First World War because, after that, "America was thus clearly Top Nation, and history came to a . [sic]"

But even after 1918, the UK retained most of its empire, and sterling retained its status as the world's reserve currency. So, the UK was still one of the most influential, if not *the* most influential, nation. It was only after the Second World War and the independence of India and most of Britain's other colonies that the UK slipped further down the pecking order. So, that is a good 100 or even 150 years of gradually sliding away from power.

However, the times are indeed a-changin', as Bob Dylan said, so looking at some of the large-scale changes that are happening right now is not a bad thing to do. For instance, the internet has changed many things. It means news now arrives instantly, no matter where it happens. It also means individual investors have direct and easy access to SEC filings and company information; people can even, in many cases, access the analyst conference call after the company's earnings release.

The internet has enabled decentralized and collaborative working. Digital nomads can now combine sun, sea, sand, and a remunerative job. Estonia has even dematerialized the nation—all government servers are duplicated offshore, a remarkable and far-sighted response to a Russian cyberattack in 2007—and now has "e-residents" establishing businesses there.

More and more computer chips are being used in cars, in white goods (large electronic products like washing machines), and in basic appliances to provide extended functionality. Self-driving cars are already with us, though so far, they haven't been given driving licenses, and the Internet of Things is likely to make our lives a good deal more linked.

The internet also consumes vast amounts of energy. It's estimated that Bitcoin consumes more electricity than either Norway or Austria. And it has created a huge cybersecurity industry because corporate dependence on digital assets is a critical vulnerability.

Looking at the war between Ukraine and Russia, you can clearly see the difference between the two types of warfare, old and new. The Russian army is traditional command and control. Ukraine, on the other hand, appears to be running a data-fueled guerilla war, using Google Maps, drones, hand-held video reconnaissance, and small teams, though it wasn't until Ukraine got HIMARS rocket launchers that the tide started turning. The jury is still out on which way things will go, but one thing is sure: the new Ukrainian army didn't give Putin a chance of taking Kyiv within seventy-two hours as he claimed he would.

This will have an impact on the world of investment. Innovation is very fast these days. In the past, major companies could maintain their leadership easily for decades, but now, the pace of change means investors need to be ready to switch their investments fast if an industry leader starts to fail. For instance, right now, there's some concern about Intel falling behind the curve, and its last set of results was poor. It was the leader in semiconductors for years, but has it lost that leadership?

Another major trend that needs to enter into any investor's thinking is the rise of China. Goldman Sachs identified the BRICs— Brazil, Russia, India, and China—but Russia's economy is structurally unsound, and Brazil has underperformed, leaving only the last two as serious competitors. India is doing well in terms of trade, but China has really made waves, becoming the world's second-largest economy and recently displaying assertiveness and even aggression in the Pacific.

China is still slightly handicapped by old attitudes and poor quality, but things are changing rapidly. It has its own versions of eBay (Alibaba) and Google (Baidu), it's making a lot of progress with electric cars, and it is getting better and better at matching Western quality and technology. It has also been investing heavily in the Belt and Road Initiative, in overland communications through Central Asia toward Kazakhstan and Turkey, and in maritime facilities in South and Southeast Asia, the Middle East, and Africa. Huge investments give China a massive amount of "soft power," though it has not always made itself popular in investee nations.

The Chinese stock market has its bulls and bears. It's been a very volatile market with some major thrills and spills along the way, and it's true that the government still runs a command economy with a little leeway for entrepreneurs rather than what it claims is "capitalism with Chinese characteristics." That's not always made investing comfortable for Westerners.

However, the Chinese economy is becoming a dominant influence in Asia and an important influence on the world economy through its involvement in offshore manufacturing facilities. (Well-known investor Jim Rogers is a huge bull of China and made the decision to have both his daughters taught Chinese from the cradle up.) China is certainly on the rise, but it isn't a major financial center per se, and its recent crackdown in Hong Kong might have been counterproductive in that regard.

Will cryptocurrency be part of the new order? Blockchain certainly will be, but it's possible that the acceptance of digital currency by central banks will end up replacing today's cryptocurrencies. The difficulty is seeing where cryptocurrency gets its value from. In the case of Bitcoin, the value was said to lie in the limited amount of BTC that could be issued; in the case of some other currencies, they're tied to "real world" assets like the dollar.

But a currency is valued by investors' and users' belief in it, which is obvious when you look at French currency during the time of the Mississippi Company. John Law simply kept printing money; when he ran out of gold to back it with, there was a run on the bank. So, any individual cryptocurrency will have value as long as people believe in its value.

Let's remember that Francis Fukuyama predicted "the end of history" back in 1992. The end of history has failed to arrive, with Al-Qaeda, the Arab Spring, and Russia's invasions of Georgia and Ukraine all trying to prove that history is alive and definitely kicking.

Will investing change? The financial instruments used and the way they are used and recorded may well change. Cash may not exist in twenty years' time. We may all be using cryptocurrency on smartphones to pay our bills. Shares in Amazon might cost $390,000 each and be traded only in fractions, or the whole stock exchange might go fractional. Crowdfunded real estate might evolve to the point that a liquid market exists in shares of apartment blocks or even single apartments, and you can buy entitlement to a quarter share of the rental or even a 1/1000th. Blockchain may mean your credit score will be real-time and will rely on tracking your bank account against your bills.

So, yes, investing might change. But the basic principles will not because they never have.

And unfortunately, many people will continue to lose money because they are not prepared to learn from the past. But if you have read this book, you will be able to think through what is happening in the world today, independently and logically, and you will most likely spot patterns that you recognize from the past.

Conclusion

This book has taken you on a whirlwind tour through history, through the world of investment, and through some basic economic concepts too. You have seen bull markets, bear markets, bubbles, and busts. We have covered wars, peace, revolutions, conquests, wealth, and poverty. But above all, you have seen the processes that are at work in human history and in stock market cycles.

These are big, long-term processes. They play out in periods of twenty, a hundred, or even two hundred years. But they're like slow, slumbering embers—a single stray spark or a breath of wind can ignite them suddenly. And they're also invisible to the people who are looking at all the short-term noise the market makes. That's like only ever reading Buzzfeed for information; you wouldn't have any idea what's really going on in the world. You have to look beneath the surface to see what's really going on.

Bubbles are almost inevitable. They can keep going long after they should have burst. But like soap bubbles, it only takes a pinprick to burst them—a single negative comment, one bad corporate result, a regulator taking unexpected action. But you'll never know when that pinprick is coming, so when you spot a bubble, just step aside.

Major investment disasters happen when too many people believe what they're told without doing their own research. Often, they are happy to believe comforting phrases like "too big to fail" because it stops them from worrying; it's like investment Prozac. Do your own research, and think for yourself. Every investor makes the occasional bad investment, but you can at least minimize the number of times you screw up.

Recessions and depressions are inevitable too. They often follow a huge credit expansion. Overleveraged businesses can't invest, overleveraged funds can't buy stocks, and overleveraged individuals have a real problem. Make sure you have an emergency fund, and don't become overextended.

It's actually possible to make money in a depression. Undervalued assets are all around. It may take a few years until they start to increase in value, but buying businesses or real estate when no one wants them can be a smart move. Letting your spare cash trickle into the stock market will pay off when the next bull market comes (and it will). Or you can start a business that helps people (or corporations) save their money.

War is the worst destroyer of wealth, far worse than a bear market or an economic downturn. In times of war, governments may move to confiscate individuals' wealth to help in the war effort or may confiscate the possessions of a targeted minority or class. For really wealthy individuals, holding assets abroad or perhaps in cryptocurrency is the best way of ensuring a positive outcome.

Those are the potential downsides, but history also shows how to maximize the upside. For instance, the story of Mansa Musa shows how education, networks, and commerce are important in the development of wealth. Empires develop in various ways, but the greatest empires have generally invested their capital in productivity, technology, and education. They have also been open to learning from other cultures.

There's no magic formula for investing profitably. But it's interesting that almost all the best-known investors have focused on a number of formulas that allow them to assess the ongoing value of the business in which they're buying shares. Not only that, but they also try to buy the shares on the cheap. It's not magic. It's a lot of hard work to find the right investments, but that's the best way to do it.

Gold rushes are like bubbles. When a new resource is found, everybody piles in. Whether it's California, the Klondike, dot coms, or Bitcoin, everyone wants a piece. But when the gold is gone, that's it—the gold rush is over. Smarter ways to play this phenomenon are to look for "picks and shovels" and sell the tools that people need or look for "real estate," such as lodging houses, saloons, data centers, or blockchain tech. When the gold rush is over, you want to have a hotel in San Francisco, not a patch of mud in the middle of nowhere.

Are we entering a new age, as some people claim? Yes and no. There are a lot of interesting things happening, but many of the basics remain the same. For instance, although the internet has enabled the birth of the digital nomad, office real estate isn't going to die overnight. People still value the chance to get together with others, to brainstorm, network, and discuss their ideas. Start-up centers like Silicon Valley aren't suddenly going to find everyone has gone to a cabin in the Yukon or an island off the coast of Thailand to work.

The basics of how bubbles work and why busts happen are still there because that's human nature.

* * *

One of the best ways to become adept at spotting the big cycles of history and markets is to read widely on history. Rather than reading popular histories that focus on kings and queens or battles and victories, read economic history and histories that track trends. The books in the bibliography are not a bad place to start. There are also plenty of free resources online that can help; many universities even put lectures online.

As well as reading history, you might benefit from reading alternative histories like Philip K. Dick's *The Man in the High Castle*, in which Germany and Japan won World War II and divided the US between them, or Kim Stanley Robinson's *Years of Rice and Salt*, which explores a world in which the Black Death killed 99 percent of Europe's population. Think up your own alternate histories; where are the inflection points? What broad trends continue in the "new" history? Can you think of other points at which history could have been changed greatly, perhaps by some small event?

Schoolteachers and historians might sniff at "alt-history," but thinking about it opens up a lot of the themes that have been discussed in this book.

What if the Wall Street Crash never happened?

What if the US adopted Bitcoin?

What if the French Revolution never happened?

What if the Confederacy had won the Civil War?

If the Wall Street Crash had not happened, volatility would have continued for some time, but the economy probably would have continued to grow. The 1930s recession might have been avoided, at least in America. But probably, this wouldn't have affected the history of Europe. One big problem from the bubble before the crash, though, is that excessive leverage was being taken on board and invested in speculative assets rather than productive assets. How would the American industry have gotten into a position to invest productively again?

If the US were to adopt Bitcoin as a legal tender, there are several interesting questions that need to be addressed. For instance, how would the relationship of BTC to dollars be managed? For Bitcoin to be used in everyday transactions, the relationship would need Bitcoin to be much more stable than it is today. Would the US seek to "own" cryptocurrency exchanges or ban US citizens from holding cryptocurrency offshore? Would the adoption of a single crypto lead to the collapse of others? And would China then launch its own official cryptocurrency?

There are not any definite answers. But the effort to think through the ramifications of these various questions is interesting. More than that, it develops the ability to think through the processes behind what the newspapers put on the front page, behind what CNN and CNBC flash up every hour. And while it won't make you rich overnight, that ability is crucial to becoming a wise and successful investor.

Here's another book by Captivating History that you might like

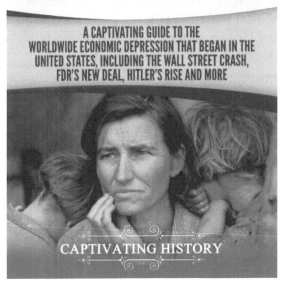

Free Bonus from Captivating History: History Ebook

Hi History Lovers!

My name is Matt Clayton, and I'm the creator of Captivating History. First off, I want to THANK YOU for reading our books in the Captivating History series. As an avid reader of History myself, I aim to produce books that will hold you captive.

Now you have a chance to join our exclusive history list so you can get the ebook below for free as well as discounts and a potential to get more history books for free! Simply click the link below to join.

P.S. If you join now, you will also receive a free Mythology book. Remember that it's 100% free to join the list.

Captivatinghistory.com/ebook

Also, make sure to follow us on:

Twitter: @Captivhistory

Facebook: Captivating History: @captivatinghistory

Youtube: Captivating History

Bibliography

Akerlof, George and Shiller, Robert J. *Phishing for Phools.* 2015.

Bellone, Benoit; de Carvalho, Raul Leote. "Value versus Glamour Stocks: The Return of Irrational Exuberance?" *The Journal of Investing.* joi.2021.1.199; DOI: https://doi.org/10.3905/joi.2021.1.199

Biggs, Barton. *Wealth, War and Wisdom.* 2008.

Brands, HW. *The Age of Gold: The Californian Gold Rush and the New American Dream.* 2002.

Condie, Richard, director: Condie, Sharon, scriptwriter. "John Law and the Mississippi Bubble." National Film Board of Canada. https://www.youtube.com/watch?v=diEVmQZ1QfM. Published 2010.

Dalio, Ray. *The Changing World Order: Why Nations Succeed and Fail.* 2021.

de Villiers, Marc and Hirtle, Sheila. *Timbuktu: The Sahara's Fabled City of Gold.* 2007.

Galbraith, JK. *The Great Crash, 1929.* 1955.

Gilman, Martin. *No Precedent, No Plan: Inside Russia's 1998 Default.* 2010.

Goldgar, Anne. *Tulipmania: Money, Honor and Knowledge in the Dutch Golden Age.* 2007.

Jorion, Philippe & Goetzmann, William N. "Global Stock Markets in the Twentieth Century." *The Journal of Finance.* Vol. 54, No.3. https://www.jstor.org/stable/222431.

Klausner, Michael and Ohlrogge, Michael. "A Sober Look at SPACs." New York University School of Law, Law and Economic Research Paper Series. Working paper no. 20-48.

Lewis, Michael. *The Big Short.* 2010.

Lynch, Peter and Rothchild, John. *Beating the Street.* 1992.

Lynch, Peter and Rothchild, John. *One Up on Wall Street.* 1989.

Mackay, Peter. *Extraordinary Popular Delusions and the Madness of Crowds.* 1841.

McCullough, Brian. *How the Internet Happened: From Netscape to the iPhone.* 2018.

McLean, Bethany and Elkind, Peter. *The Smartest Guys in the Room: The Amazing Rise and Scandalous Fall of Enron.* 2003.

Moser, Petra; Voena, Alessandra; Waldinger, Fabian. "German-Jewish Émigrés and US Invention." *The American Economic Review.* Vol. 104, No. 10. 2013.

Nations, Scott. *A History of the United States in Five Crashes: Stock Market Meltdowns That Defined a Nation.* 2017.

Quinn and Turner. *Boom and Bust: A Global History of Financial Bubbles.* 2020.

Rosen, Fred. *Gold! The Story of the 1848 Gold Rush and How It Shaped a Nation.* 2005.

Rothschild archive. https://www.rothschildarchive.org/business/n_m_rothschild_and_sons_london/nathan_mayer_rothschild_and_waterloo.

Smith, Mark B. *A History of the Global Stock Market: From Ancient Rome to Silicon Valley.* 2004.

Swedroe, Larry E and Balaban, RC. *Investment Mistakes Even Smart Investors Make and How to Avoid Them.* 2011.

Temin, Peter. *Lessons from the Great Depression.* 1989.

Walsh, Justyn. *Investing with Keynes: How the World's Greatest Economist Overturned Conventional Wisdom and Made a Fortune on the Stock Market.* 2008.

Weatherford, Jack. *The History of Money.* 1997.

Woolmer, Christopher. *Fire and Steam: A New History of the Railways in Britain.* 2008.

Made in United States
Troutdale, OR
09/04/2024

22585430R10066